Indian Vegetarian Delicacies

Indian Vegetarian Delicacies

Sudha Mathur

Ocean Books Pvt. Ltd.
ISO 9001:2015 Publishers

Published by

Ocean Books (P) Ltd.

4/19 Asaf Ali Road,
New Delhi-110 002 (INDIA)
e-mail: info@oceanbooks.in

ISBN 81-87100-30-3
INDIAN VEGETARIAN DELICACIES

Edition
2024

Price
₹ 500.00 (Rupees Five Hundred only)

Photographs
S. Kumar

Printed at
Narula Printers, Delhi

CONTENTS

Soups

Salad

Raite aur Bade

Daalein aur Karhi

Sabzian

Roti-Chawal-Pulao

Naashte

Dessert

CREAM OF TOMATO SOUP

INGREDIENTS :

1 kg tomatoes (chopped)
½ cup *garam masala* (whole) (black pepper, cloves, cinnamon and black cardamoms)
1 tbsp sugar
1 tsp salt
½ cup cream (beaten)
1 tsp green coriander (finely chopped)

METHOD :

1. Puree tomatoes, strain juice and heat it on medium flame.
2. Coarsely grind *garam masala*, tie it in fine muslin and drop it into the simmering soup.
3. Allow soup to thicken, meanwhile gently squeeze spice bundle with a ladle or spoon so as to release the flavour into the simmering soup. Repeat this a number of times, as this will enhance both taste and aroma of the soup.
4. Remove from heat and stir in sugar and salt.
5. Serve it piping hot in bowls, topped with a spoon of beaten cream and sprinkle with coriander.
6. This soup can be accompanied with golden fried or baked bread croutons.

TOMATO AND VEGETABLE SOUP

INGREDIENTS :

750 grams tomatoes (chopped)
2-3 onions (finely chopped)
2 cloves of garlic (crushed)
1 cucumber (chopped into 1½" sticks)
1 capsicum (chopped)
1 cup cabbage (shredded)
2 tbsp butter
¾ tsp salt
½ tsp black pepper (freshly ground)
1 tbsp cornflour

METHOD :

1. Heat butter in a heavy bottomed pan, add onions and garlic and stir-fry until golden brown. Add tomatoes and cook till done.
2. Turn off the fire and strain stock. Again turn on the heat and allow the stock to simmer.
3. Add rest of the vegetables and cook for 5 mts and add salt to it.
4. Make cornflour paste by dissolving it in a cup of water, add it to the simmering soup and stir till it thickens.
5. Add pepper and serve steaming hot.
6. You can also add quartered boiled eggs.

MUSHROOM SOUP

INGREDIENTS :

250 grams mushrooms (fresh and large, quartered)
2-3 fresh spring onions (chopped)
1 tbsp butter
½ tsp each salt and pepper
2 tbsp thick tomato puree
4 cups mix vegetable stock
½ tsp sugar
1½ tbsp refined flour
2-3 cloves of garlic (crushed) (optional)

METHOD :

1. Heat butter and stir-fry onions and garlic till golden brown.
2. Add mushrooms and stir-fry again.
3. Sprinkle flour and stir-fry till golden pink and add salt.
4. Stir in tomato puree and stock and allow it to simmer for a few mts.
5. Turn off the heat and allow it to cool.
6. Puree the soup and reheat before serving.
7. Top it with cream and serve piping hot with buttered buns.

BEANS SOUP

INGREDIENTS :

¼ cup kidney beans (whole)
¼ cup Bengal gram (whole)
¼ cup black eye beans (whole)
¼ cup large white gram (whole)
2 cups tomato juice
1 onion (finely chopped)
1 tbsp butter
1 tsp salt
½ tsp pepper (freshly ground)
¼ cup cream
½ tbsp green coriander (finely chopped)

METHOD :

1. Clean and wash all the beans and gram and soak overnight.
2. Next morning, heat butter and stir-fry onions till golden brown.
3. Add the soaked beans (unstrained) and salt and boil till done.
4. Stir in tomato juice and pepper.
5. Turn off the heat and serve hot topped with whipped cream and coriander.
6. Serve with buttered toasts or rusks.

APPLE AND CABBAGE SOUP

INGREDIENTS :

4 apples
3 cups cabbage (shredded)
1 cup tomato juice
1 potato
1 onion (finely chopped)
1 clove of garlic
1½ tbsp butter
1 tsp salt
½ tsp black pepper (freshly ground)
¼ cup cream
fried pieces of *makhana* and bread croutons

METHOD :

1. Wash, cut and core the apples, peel and cut potatoes into pieces.
2. Heat butter in a heavy-bottomed pan and fry the onions, garlic and vegetables till they are pink and tender.
3. Add four cups of water and bring to a boil. Stir in tomato juice and allow the soup to cool. Blend in a blender when cold.
4. Before serving, reheat the thick soup. Sprinkle salt and pepper and spoon puffed cream on top.
5. Decorate with *makhanas* and croutons and serve hot.

P.S. : puffed lotus seeds are called *makhanas*.

COCONUT AND VEGETABLE SOUP

INGREDIENTS :

1 fresh coconut (grated)
1 cup white gourd (chopped)
1 cup tomato (chopped)
¼ cup beetroot (chopped)
1 cup spinach (finely chopped)
¼ cup cottage cheese (*paneer*) (grated)
½ tsp black pepper powder
1 tomato (finely chopped)
salt to taste

METHOD :

1. Boil chopped gourd, chopped tomatoes, beetroot and half the spinach in 4 cups of water and salt.
2. Strain the stock.
3. Boil grated coconut in one and a half glass of water. Blend in a mixer and strain out coconut milk.
4. Add coconut milk to the vegetable stock and bring it to a boil.
5. Add finely chopped tomatoes, rest of the spinach, and cottage cheese to the boiling soup. Boil for another few mts and allow the spinach to soften and tenderize.
6. Sprinkle salt and serve piping hot with bread and butter.

KHIRE KA THANDA SOUP

INGREDIENTS :

For soup :

2 fresh cucumbers (large)
½ cup cottage cheese (*paneer*) (grated)
1 potato (boiled)
2 spring onions
3 tbsp lemon juice
½ cup fresh cream
2 cups water
1 tbsp green coriander and mint (finely chopped)
¾ tsp salt
½ tsp pepper (freshly ground)

For tomato ice :

2 cups fresh tomato juice
2½ tsp sugar
¾ tsp salt

METHOD :

1. Peel and grate cucumbers and potato.
2. Chop spring onion and keep aside.
3. Boil the vegetables and lemon juice in 2 cups of water, add salt to it and allow it to cool.
4. Blend the cold soup in a blender and refrigerate.
5. Before serving sprinkle pepper and herbs.
6. Decorate with tomato ice and serve chilled.
7. To make tomato ice, combine all the ingredients and blend. Set and freeze to ice cubes. Use as cubes or crushed.

SOUP CHAAWALI

INGREDIENTS :

1 turnip (small)
3 carrots (medium)
2 spring onions
1 cup cauliflower florets
½ cup cottage cheese (grated)
½ cup noodles (boiled)
½ cup rice (boiled and salted)
½ cup cheese (grated) (cheddar)
2 cups tomato juice
1½ tsp salt
½ tsp black pepper (freshly ground)
1 tbsp butter
¾ tbsp refined flour

METHOD :

1. Peel and finely chop potatoes and turnip and coarsely chop the spring onion.
2. Heat butter in a heavy bottomed pan, sprinkle flour and stir-fry till pink.
3. Add tomato juice along with 5-6 cups of water and bring to a boil.
4. To the boiling soup, add salt, pepper and chopped vegetables, and cook till the vegetables are done.
5. Add grated cottage cheese, noodles and salted rice to it and cook for another few mts.
6. Sprinkle grated cheddar cheese, turn off the heat and serve the wholesome soup piping hot.

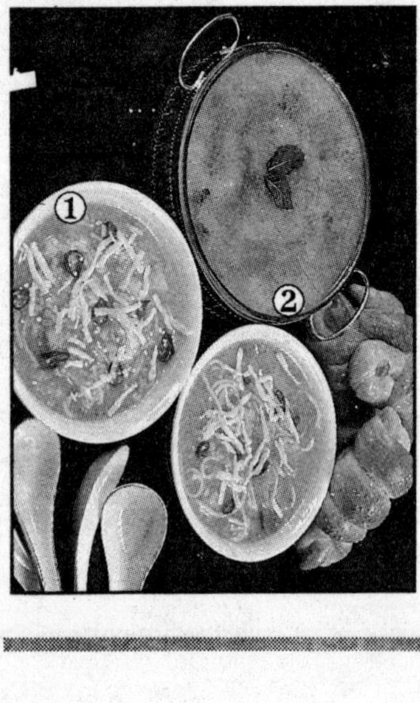

① Soup Chaawali—p. 16
② Khire ka Thanda Soup—p. 15

FALOAN KA THANDA SOUP

(cold mixed fruit soup)

INGREDIENTS :

½ kg cherries (pitted) or pineapple (cleaned and eyed) or plums (pitted) or a combination of these fruits (chopped)
4 cups water
¾ cups sugar (can be adjusted according to the sourness of fruits)
1 tbsp lemon juice
1 cup curd (fresh and thick)
10-12 leaves (mint and green coriander)
crushed ice

METHOD :

1. Boil the chopped fruits in sugar and water till they are done. Turn off the heat and allow to cool.
2. Stir in lemon juice and blend in a blender.
3. Serve chilled topped with chilled curd, crushed ice and herbs.

① Faloan ka Thanda Soup—p. 19
② Hariyala Soup—p. 20

HARIYALA SOUP

INGREDIENTS :

250 grams spinach
4-5 salad leaves
1 cup peas (shelled)
1 potato (boiled)
3-4 fresh spring onions (onion and stem separated)
2½ cups water
1½ tbsp butter
1½ cups cream (puffed)
1 tbsp green coriander and mint (finely chopped)
1½ tbsp lemon juice
½ tsp salt
½ tsp pepper

METHOD :

1. Shred the spinach, salad leaves and spring onion stems and make a fine paste of shelled peas.
2. Heat butter in a heavy bottomed pan, add finely chopped onion and stir-fry till pink.
3. Add the chopped greens, grated potato and roll in butter.
4. Stir in the pea paste, water, salt and pepper and boil for 10-15 mts, turn off the heat and allow cooling.
5. Blend in a mixer when cold.
6. Before serving boil once and serve hot topped with puffed cream and chopped herbs. Sprinkle lemon juice on top.

SALAD

ANKURIT (SPROUTED) SALAD

INGREDIENTS :

1 cup green gram (*moong dal*) (sprouted)
1 cup motth gram (*motth*) (sprouted)
1 cup soyabean (sprouted)
1 cup onion (finely chopped)
1 tomato (finely chopped)
2-3 fresh green chillies (finely chopped)
1 potato (boiled and chopped)
salt, pepper and lemon juice to taste

METHOD :

1. Steam the sprouts till done.
2. In a salad bowl combine the steamed sprouts and chopped vegetables.
3. Sprinkle lemon juice, salt and pepper, toss and serve the nutritious salad.

Finely chopped mixed seasonal salad vegetables (carrot, radish, cucumber, etc) can be added, if desired.

TILSHAD SALAD

INGREDIENTS :

1 apple
1 cup shredded cabbage
2 potatoes (boiled, cubed and tossed in hot oil)
2 sweet potatoes (boiled or roasted)
1 cup pineapple pieces
½ cup sesame seeds (roasted) *(til)*
¼ tbsp refined oil
½ tsp sugar (powdered)
½ tsp lemon or sweet lime juice
salt and pepper to taste
salad leaves (to cover the salad platter)

METHOD :

1. Chop apples. Peel and chop potatoes and sweet potatoes.
2. Wash salad leaves and spread them on the platter.
3. Combine chopped fruits and vegetables in a bowl.
4. Mix the sesame seeds with oil and sprinkle over the top.
5. To the lemon/sweet lime juice add sugar, salt and pepper.
6. Sprinkle on the salad and toss with a delicate hand.
7. Arrange on the platter and serve.

CHURRI SALAD

INGREDIENTS :

2 radish (fresh and large)
2 carrots (fresh and large)
5-6 green chillies (finely chopped)
½" piece of ginger (grated)
2 tomatoes (large and finely chopped)
3 tbsp lemon juice
salt and pepper to taste

METHOD :

1. Grate radish and carrot and apply gentle pressure to remove excess water.
2. Combine all the grated ingredients in a bowl or arrange in a pattern on a platter.
3. Add salt, pepper and chopped chillies to the lemon juice and sprinkle on top of salad and serve.

For the hot toothed sprinkle ½ tsp ground red pepper or paprika.

JELLY CRYSTAL SALAD

INGREDIENTS :

½ cup pineapple pieces
½ cup orange/mango pieces
½ cup grapes (halved)
½ cup carrot and radish/ cucumber pieces
½ cup pomegranate seeds
1 banana (chopped)
1 large tomato (chopped)
2 lemons
1 packet jelly (any flavour)
1 tbsp green coriander (finely chopped)
salt and pepper to taste

METHOD :

1. Prepare jelly according to the directions on the packet but do not allow to set.
2. Add salt, pepper and lemon juice to it.
3. Chop all the fruits and vegetables and add to the liquid jelly.
4. Moisten a bowl or a jelly mould, pour in the fruity jelly and allow to set.
5. Serve chilled.

NOODLES CRUNCH SALAD

INGREDIENTS :

1 cup noodles (crisp fried)
1 cup cottage cheese (cubed and fried till pink)
1 cup potato chips
1 cup peas (shelled)
½ cup fresh coconut pieces (white part)
6-7 salted biscuits (broken to pieces)
1 cucumber (chopped)
1 potato (boiled and chopped)
1 tomato (chopped)
1 spring onion (fresh and chopped)
2 tbsp tomato sauce
1 capsicum (chopped)
1 tbsp cheese spread
½ tbsp green chilli sauce/ *dhaniya chutney*
1 tbsp butter
salt and pepper to taste

METHOD :

1. Combine tomato sauce, chilli sauce and cheese to form dressing.
2. Heat butter in a pan and stir-fry onions, capsicum, potato and peas. Add rest of the vegetables, give it a toss and remove from heat.
3. Add crisp noodles, biscuits and coconut and arrange on a platter.
4. Border the platter with potato chips, sprinkle salt, pepper and dressing on top and serve.

DAHI (CURD) SALAD

INGREDIENTS :

1½ cup fresh curd
1 tbsp fresh coriander (finely chopped)
1 tbsp fresh mint (finely chopped)
1 tomato (large)
2-3 green chillies (finely chopped)
¾ cup seasonal salad vegetables
2 large potatoes (boiled and diced)
½ cup cottage cheese *(paneer)* (diced)
salt and pepper to taste

METHOD :

1. Blend the curd along with the herbs in a blender.
2. Chop tomatoes and add them to diced potato and *paneer.*
3. Chop the vegetables and combine everything except curd and seasonings in a large bowl.
4. Add the herb curd and sprinkle salt, pepper and chopped chillies on top.
5. Toss the salad with delicate hand and serve.

BEANS SALAD

INGREDIENTS :

¼ cup kidney beans
¼ cup black-eyed beans
¼ cup black gram
¼ cup large white gram
½ cup milk
½ cup processed cheese (grated)
2 tbsp refined flour
1 tbsp butter
2 tbsp green coriander and mint (chopped)
lemon juice, chopped green chillies, salt and pepper to taste

METHOD :

1. Clean and wash the beans and grams and soak them overnight.
2. Next morning, add salt and boil them, till tender, in the soaking water itself taking care that they remain whole.
3. Heat butter in a pan, sprinkle flour and stir-fry till pink. Turn down the heat and slowly stir in the milk to prepare white sauce while taking care that no lumps are formed. Add salt to it.
4. Stir in the grated cheese and cook till it melts.
5. Turn off the heat and allow the sauce to cool.
6. When cold add the boiled seeds and tumble mix with a gentle hand.
7. Arrange in a serving dish and sprinkle coriander, mint, chillies, salt, pepper and lemon juice on top.

SABZIKAS SALAD

INGREDIENTS :

1 beetroot
2 onions
2 cucumbers
2 lean cucumbers
4-6 tomatoes
2 potatoes (boiled)
2 lemons
½ cup cottage cheese *(paneer)* (fresh)
4-6 fresh salad leaves (medium-sized)
salt and pepper to taste

METHOD :

1. Finely dice the onion.
2. Grate cucumbers and potatoes. Also grate beetroot and keep it separate.
3. Wash and clean the tomatoes, slice out their tops and scoop out the pulp.
4. Stuff the tomatoes with grated vegetables.
6. Put a little grated beetroot on it.
7. Crumble the cottage cheese and add salt and pepper to it. Use a little on top of every tomato.
8. Juice the scooped out pulp and add lemon juice to it.
9. Arrange the stuffed tomatoes, remaining grated vegetables and *paneer* on a salad platter lined with salad leaves.
10. Just before serving sprinkle the mixed juice on top.

CREAMY SALAD

INGREDIENTS :

2 large onions (sliced)
2 large radish (cubed lengthwise)
2 large carrot (cubed lengthwise)
2 fresh tomatoes (chopped)
½ cup cottage cheese *(paneer)* (diced)
½ cup banana (pieces)
3-4 green chillies (chopped lengthwise)
½ cup pineapple (pieces)
½ cup papaya (pieces)
½ tbsp processed cheese (grated)
2 cups fresh cream
1½ tbsp mint (finely chopped)
salt and pepper to taste

METHOD :

1. Season the cream with salt and pepper and stir in the chopped mint.
2. Arrange all the ingredients on a salad platter.
3. Pour the seasoned cream evenly on top, mix with a gentle hand and serve.

PASTA SALAD

INGREDIENTS :

½ cup macaroni (boiled)
½ cup peas (shelled)
8-10 button mushrooms (quartered and lightly fried)
1 cucumber (finely diced)
1 beetroot (juliennes)
1½ cup peanuts (roasted and shelled)
1 capsicum (shredded and stir-fried)
1 large spring onion (chopped)
6 cabbage leaves (large whole)
2 tbsp oil
2 tbsp vinegar
1 tbsp lemon juice
2 tbsp onion paste
½ cup processed cheese (grated)
2 tbsp honey

METHOD :

1. Combine oil, vinegar, lemon juice, honey and onion paste to make the dressing. Season it with salt and pepper.
2. Combine macaroni, peas, mushrooms, cucumber, beetroot, onion and capsicum in a bowl.
3. Pour in the dressing and tumble mix the salad gently.
4. Arrange the crisp cabbage leaves on the platter and the curved leaves as cups, fill them with the prepared mixture.
5. Sprinkle grated cheese on top and serve the individual cups.

RAITE AUR BADE

(Curd preparations)

HARE-BHARE DAHI BADE

INGREDIENTS :

1 cup green gram *(moong dal)*
3 cups black gram *(urad dal)*
1¾ cups fresh green coriander (chopped)
2-3 green chillies (finely chopped)
½" piece ginger (finely chopped)
¼ tsp asafoetida
¾ tsp salt
½ tsp red pepper or paprika (powder)
thick churned curd
tamarind sauce *(saunth)*
oil for frying

For garnishing :

Red pepper, yellow pepper, black pepper (all powdered), roasted and powdered cummin seeds, finely chopped coriander, green chillies, grated ginger

METHOD :

1. Soak the pulses overnight, grind washed pulses, coriander, asafoetida, salt and red pepper to make *pitthi.*
2. Gently whisk the *pitthi* with a spatula in-between giving a few dashes of water. Periodically, put *pitthi* in a pan full of water and see if it floats. Keep whisking till the *pitthi* floats. Now heat oil in a *karahi* or wok.
3. On a flat surface spread a fine muslin (moistened). Put *pitthi* on it and flatten with a moist gentle hand. Put some of the chopped green chilli and ginger in the centres.
4. Now, gently, using the underlying cloth, enclose the chilli and ginger into the *pitthi* and seal using a moist hand.
5. Deep fry in hot oil and remove to a bowl filled with water as this allows the *badas* to remain soft.
6. Whisk curd and salt in a bowl. Before serving, gently squeeze out the excess water, dip in the curd and arrange the *badas* on a flat shallow serving dish.

   P.S. : Put only as much red and yellow pepper as your guests can take.

DAHI PAKORI

INGREDIENTS :

4 cup green gram *(moong dal)*
1 tbsp ginger paste
a pinch of asafoetida
¾ tsp salt
½ tsp red pepper
oil for frying
¼ cup raisins
4 green chillies (finely chopped)
sugar, salt, red pepper (powder) and roasted cummin seeds
curd (thick, smooth and slightly soured) (as required)
hot and spicy potato *latchaa* (fried potato juliennes)

METHOD :

1. Clean, wash and soak the *dal* overnight. Next morning drain and grind along with salt, ginger paste and red pepper powder to make *pitthi.*
2. Add chopped chillies and raisins to it and whisk.
3. Heat oil in a *karahi* or wok.
4. Put spoonfuls of *pitthi* into hot oil and deep-fry the *pakoris* till golden brown. Remove in a bowl of water.
5. Squeeze out excess water.
6. Add salt and sugar to the curd and whisk.
7. Add the squeezed *pakoris* to the curd.
8. Sprinkle the spices and crumbled chips on top and serve.

HARA-BHARA RAITA

INGREDIENTS :

4 cups curd

2 cups spinach or *bathua* leaves (blanched, squeezed and ground to paste)

½ cup shelled peas (fresh and tender)

1 tbsp fresh green coriander (chopped)

¼ tsp cummin seeds

1½ tsp butter

a pinch of asafoetida

½ tsp cummin seeds (roasted and powdered)

¾ tsp salt

½ tsp red chilli powder

1 dry red chilli

METHOD :

1. Whisk the curd and spinach/*bathua* paste in a bowl.
2. Add salt and mix well.
3. Stir in the peas, coriander, cummin powder and red chilli powder.
4. To prepare tempering, heat butter, add dried chilli, cummin seeds and asafoetida and allow to crackle.
5. Turn off the heat, sprinkle evenly on top of the *raita* and cover immediately.
6. After 2-3 mts remove the lid and serve.

SHAHI RAITA

INGREDIENTS :

4 cups fresh curd
1 cup lotus seed puffs (*makhana*) (halved)
¼ cup musk melon seeds and *chiraunji*
¼ cup cashew nuts and almonds (chopped)
2-3 green chillies (chopped)
1 tbsp green coriander (finely chopped)
salt to taste
½ tsp cummin seeds (roasted and powdered)
¼ tsp red chilli powder
¼ cup pure *ghee*
¼ cup coconut water

METHOD :

1. Heat *ghee* in a frying pan and stir-fry the dry fruits to pink.
2. In the left over *ghee*, stir-fry *makhanas* till golden.
3. Churn the curd along with salt and coconut water.
4. Before serving add all the dry fruits and *makhanas* to the curd.
5. Garnish the *raita* with chopped green chillies, coriander, cummin powder and red chilli powder.
6. Serve the delicious and rich *shahi raita*.

This *raita* should be consumed within an hour or so as it has a low shelf life since the dry fruits become soggy if kept for a long time in curd.

① Beans Salad—p. 27
② Sabzikas Salad—p. 28

FALOAN KA RAITA

INGREDIENTS :

2 cups chopped mixed fruits (pineapple, grapes, bananas and other seasonal fruits)
4-6 cups fresh curd
½ cup cream
2 tbsp fruit juice (any from the above)
1½ tsp lemon juice
1½ tsp sugar
¾ tsp salt
½ tsp red chilli powder
½ tsp cummin seeds (roasted)
1 tbsp green coriander (finely chopped)
1 tbsp green chillies (finely chopped)

METHOD :

1. Fold chopped fruits in sugar and lemon juice.
2. Churn curd with salt and fruit juice.
3. Add the sweet and sour fruits to the curd.
4. Garnish with red chilli powder, cummin seeds, coriander and green chillies.
5. Chill and top with puffed cream before serving.

① Creamy Salad—p. 29
② Pasta Salad—p. 30

DAHI KI GUJHIA

INGREDIENTS :

For *gujhia* :

4 cups black gram *(urad dhuli dal)* (washed and skinned)
½ cup coconut (dry and grated)
¼ cup raisins, *chiraunji* and almond (chopped)
¼ tsp asafoetida
½" piece of ginger
3-4 green chillies
¾ tsp salt
½ tsp red chilli powder
oil for frying
4-6 cups thick curd

As accompaniments :

whole white gram *(kabuli chana)* (boiled)
potatoes (boiled and finely diced)
green coriander (finely chopped)
cummin seeds (roasted-powdered)
red chilli powder
white pepper powder
salt, tamarind sauce *(saunth)*
coriander *chutney*

METHOD :

1. Wash *dal* and soak overnight.
2. Next morning wash again and grind along with salt, red chilli powder, green chillies, ginger and asafoetida to make *pitthi*.
3. Combine all the dry fruits and grated coconut. Heat oil and then turn the flame to medium.
4. On a flat surface spread a fine muslin (moistened). Spoon about 1½ tbsp *pitthi* on it and flatten with a moist delicate hand.
5. Put a little of the dry fruit mixture in the centre. Now, gently, using the underlying cloth, fold the *pitthi* disc, one half over the other, to form a semi-circular *gujhia* enclosing the dry fruits.
6. Seal the edges with a moist hand and deep fry in hot oil.
7. Fry the *gujhia* till golden pink and remove to a bowl of water as this allows the *gujhia* to remain soft. Similarly fry *gujhia* from rest of the *pitthi*.
8. Gently squeeze out water so that *gujhia* is not broken. Add salt to the curd and churn it till smooth.
9. Dip *gujhia* in the curd and arrange in a shallow serving platter.
10. Pour remaining curd evenly to cover *gujhias*.
11. Garnish with a little of coriander *chutney, saunth,* potatoes, boiled *chana,* spices, chillies and coriander and serve.

JELLY CRYSTAL RAITA

INGREDIENTS :

4 cups curd (strained)
½ packet strawberry jelly
½ tsp cummin seeds (roasted)
½ tbsp sugar
1 tsp lemon juice
1 tbsp green coriander (finely chopped)
1 tsp salt

METHOD :

1. Prepare jelly according to the directions on the packet.
2. Add lemon juice to it and refrigerate to set in patterned ice trays.
3. Churn the curd along with salt.
4. De-mould the jelly cubes when set and decorate in the curd bowl.
5. Sprinkle roasted cummin seeds and chopped coriander on top and serve chilled.

PING-PONG RAITA

INGREDIENTS :

250 grams fresh cottage cheese *(paneer)*
1 cup orange/sweet lime/pineapple (cleaned, seeded, eyed and chopped)
½ tbsp green coriander (finely chopped)
½ tsp black pepper (freshly ground)
a pinch of sugar
4 cups curd
1 tsp *chaat masala*
1 tsp mint (finely chopped)
salt to taste
oil for frying

METHOD :

1. Crumble the cheese and mash with pepper and sugar.
2. Shape medium-sized balls and deep fry to pink.
3. Remove on kitchen/brown paper so that the paper soaks excess oil.
4. Add salt to the curd and churn.
5. Stir in chopped fruits, fried cheese-balls and chopped mint and coriander.
6. Sprinkle *chaat masala* on top and serve.

NAMKEEN KA RAITA

INGREDIENTS :

4 cups curd (strained)
½ cup spicy *mogra*
½ cup *dal-motth*
½ cup spicy peanuts
½ cup fine *sev (namkeen)*
½ tsp mint paste
½ tsp cummin seeds (roasted and powdered)
¾ tsp salt
2-3 green chillies (finely chopped)
green coriander (finely chopped) for garnishing

METHOD :

1. Add salt, mint paste and roasted cummin seeds to the curd and churn.
2. Combine all the *namkeen* in separate bowl.
3. Just before serving add *namkeen* to the churned curd and garnish with chopped coriander and chillies.

CHINAURI AUR ANAAR KA RAITA

INGREDIENTS :

1½ cup fine *chinauri (besani boondi)*
1 cup pomegranate seeds
½ cup onion (finely chopped) (optional)
2-3 green chillies (finely chopped)
4 cups curd (smooth and thick)
½ tsp cummin seeds (roasted-powdered)
½ tsp red chillies (dried and powdered)
1 tsp salt
a pinch of mustard
a few curry leaves
½ tsp *ghee* or oil

METHOD :

1. Whisk the curd in a bowl. Whisk-in salt and a few dashes of water to get the desired consistency.
2. Stir in *chinauri,* pomegranate, onion and green chillies.
3. Garnish the top with cummin and red chilli powder.
4. To prepare tempering, heat oil and then allow it to cool. Add mustard and curry leaves and allow to crackle.
5. When it starts crackling, use it to temper the *raita*.
6. Serve the tempered aromatic *raita*.

DAALEIN AUR KARHI

(Dals and Karhies)

SHAHI URAD-CHANA SPECIAL

INGREDIENTS :

1 cup black gram *(urad dhuli)* (washed and skinned)
1 cup Bengal gram *(chana dal)*
1 onion (chopped)
2 dried red chillies
½" piece of ginger (ground)
a pinch of asafoetida
1 tsp salt
¼ tsp turmeric powder
½ tsp red chilli powder
1 tbsp musk melon seeds (stir fried)
1 tbsp pure *ghee*

METHOD :

1. Soak both *dals* for half an hour.
2. Rub the soaked dal in-between your palms to clean it and wash.
3. Add ginger paste, salt, turmeric powder, asafoetida, red chilli powder and about five cups of water and pressure cook for 5 mts. Take care that the gram remains intact.
4. Heat *ghee* in a pan, add dried chillies to it and allow to crackle.
5. Now add chopped onion and stir-fry till pink. Keep aside some of it.
6. Add boiled *dal* to the cooking onions and cook for further 5 mts.
7. Convert to a serving dish and sprinkle fried onion and melon seeds on top.
8. Serve this special *dal* with hot-soft *chapaties* and pickle.

MASALA LAUKI AUR CHANA DAL

INGREDIENTS :

2 cups white gourd *(lauki)* (chopped)
1½ cups Bengal gram *(chana dal)* (washed and skinned)
1 tbsp pure *ghee*
¼ tsp asafoetida
¼ tsp cummin seeds
3-4 cloves
3-4 bay leaf
¼ tsp turmeric powder
½ tsp red chilli powder
¾ tsp salt
2 green chillies (finely chopped)
1 lemon

METHOD :

1. Wash and soak *dal* for about half an hour.
2. Rub the soaked *dal* in-between your palms.
3. Pressure cook *dal* in water (4 cups), salt, red chilli powder and turmeric powder.
4. Add the chopped gourd and pressure cook till done.
5. For tempering, heat *ghee* in a pan, add cloves, bay leaf, asafoetida and cummin seeds and allow to crackle.
6. Add boiled *dal* to the pan and simmer to desired consistency.
7. Serve hot topped with chopped green chillies and lemon juice.

SABZ ARHAR

INGREDIENTS :

2 cups red gram *(arhar dal)*
3 cups chopped mixed vegetables (white gourd, peas, tomato, spinach, cauliflower, green chillies, onion) and cottage cheese *(paneer)*
1 tsp salt
¼ tsp turmeric powder
½ tsp red chilli powder
½ tsp dried mango *(amchoor)* powder
1 tbsp pure *ghee*
¼ tsp asafoetida
¼ tsp cummin seeds
¼ tsp mustard seeds
2 cloves of garlic
2 red chillies (dried)
1 tbsp lemon juice

METHOD :

1. Wash *dal,* soak it for half an hour and wash again.
2. Add salt, spices, chopped vegetables and five cups of water and pressure cook till done.
3. Take care that the vegetables are crunchy and not overcooked.
4. Heat *ghee* in a pan, add garlic and dried chillies and allow to crackle.
5. Add cooked *dal* to it and cook for a few mts.
6. Sprinkle lemon juice on top. Serve hot with rice and pickles.

SAABUT MOONG PANEERI

INGREDIENTS :

2 cups green gram *(moong dal)*
100 grams cottage cheese *(paneer)* (cubed)
1 tbsp pure *ghee*
1 tsp salt
¼ tsp turmeric powder
½ tsp red chilli powder
2 tomatoes (juiced)
1 onion (finely chopped)
2 cloves of garlic (crushed)
1 tbsp ginger paste
1-2 red chillies (dried)
a pinch of asafoetida
1 tbsp green coriander (finely chopped)

METHOD :

1. Wash, soak *dal* for an hour and wash again.
2. Add salt, turmeric powder, red chilli powder and asafoetida to it and pressure cook till done.
3. Heat *ghee* in a pan, add dried chillies and allow to crackle.
4. Add onions, garlic and ginger and stir-fry till onion turns golden brown.
5. Add tomatoes and cook till reddish colour appears.
6. Add cubed *paneer,* fold in the gravy and cook covered for a few mts.
7. Add the cooked *dal* to it, cover and cook for another 5 mts.
8. Remove the cover and cook for a few more mts. This will give *dal* a characteristic aroma.
9. Sprinkle coriander on top and serve hot with buttered *chapaties* and coriander *chutney.*

URAD MUSHROOM

INGREDIENTS :

1 cup black gram *(urad dal)* (washed and skinned)
100 gram button mushroom
2 red chillies (dried)
a pinch of asafoetida
1" piece of ginger (julienne)
1 tsp salt
½ tsp turmeric powder
1 tbsp pure *ghee*
1 onion (medium-sized)
1 tsp black pepper (freshly ground)

METHOD :

1. Wash *dal* and soak for about 2 hours.
2. Wash the soaked *dal* again and continue washing till the run-down water becomes clear.
3. Add turmeric, salt, asafoetida and 1½ cup of water to it and pressure cook for 5-7 mts or till done.
4. Take the lid off and cook till all the water evaporates.
5. Peel, half and slice the onions.
6. Heat *ghee* in a pan and stir-fry the onions to pink.
7. Add button mushrooms to it and stir-fry till done.
8. Add dried chillies to it and allow to crackle.
9. Add the cooked *dal* and pepper to it and mix well.
10. Serve hot garnished with ginger juliennes.

NUTRI MASOOR

INGREDIENTS :

1 cup nutri-nuggets (soya-nuggets) (coarsely ground and soaked)
1½ cups lentil *(masoor dal)*
¾ tsp salt
¼ tsp turmeric powder
½ tsp red chilli powder
1 tbsp pure *ghee*
¼ cup tomato pulp
¼ tsp asafoetida
¼ tsp cummin seeds

METHOD :

1. Wash *dal* and soak for about ½ an hour.
2. Heat *ghee* in a pan, add asafoetida and cummin seeds and allow to crackle.
3. Add salt, red chilli powder, turmeric powder and ¼ cup of water to it and cook.
4. Add soaked nuggets and stir-fry till combined.
5. Add tomato pulp, mix well and allow to boil.
6. Now add the soaked *dal* and stir well.
7. Add 5-6 cups of water and pressure cook for 5-10 mts.
8. Turn off the heat, remove the lid and mix well.
9. Serve piping hot with rice and curd.

GHUTWAAN MOONG

INGREDIENTS :

2 cups green gram *(moong chhilka)*
2 large onions (finely chopped)
1 large tomato (finely chopped)
¾ tsp salt
½ tsp turmeric powder
½ tsp red chilli powder
¼ tsp grated ginger
1 tbsp pure *ghee*
2 red chillies (dried)
a pinch of asafoetida

METHOD :

1. Clean, wash and soak *dal* for half an hour.
2. Add salt, turmeric powder and red chilli powder to it and cook.
3. Add grated ginger and chopped vegetables to it and pressure cook till done.
4. To prepare the tempering, heat *ghee* in a pan, add asafoetida and dried chillies to it and allow to crackle.
5. Temper *dal* with the tempering and cook for further 5 mts.
6. Serve hot garnished with green chillies and lemon juice.

MOONG AHLAN

INGREDIENTS :

2 cups green gram *(moong dal dhuli)* (washed and skinned)
2 cups spinach
1 cup tomatoes (finely chopped)
¼ cup gram flour
1 tsp salt
½ tsp turmeric powder
¾ tsp red chilli powder
2 tbsp pure *ghee*
2 red chillies (dried)
¼ tsp asafoetida
¼ tsp cummin seeds
1 onion (finely chopped)
2-3 green chillies (finely chopped)
2-3 cloves of garlic (crushed) (optional)
lemon juice for taste

METHOD :

1. Wash *dal* and soak it for half an hour.
2. Wash again, drain and add salt, red chilli powder, turmeric powder, spinach, chopped tomatoes and 4 cups of water and pressure cook till done.
3. Mix well so as to give it a uniform texture.
4. Dissolve the flour in ¼ cup of water and add to the cooked *dal*. Keep stirring so that the flour does not stick to the bottom and allow the *dal* to thicken. Keep the flame below medium.
5. When a characteristic aroma starts rising, turn the flame to low.
6. Heat *ghee* in a pan, add onions, garlic and dried chillies to it and allow it to crackle.
7. When the onions turn pink, add asafoetida and cummin seeds to it and allow to crackle.
8. Pour the cooking *dal* into it, mix well and cover for half a minute.
9. Pour lemon juice on top and serve the delicious *dal* with *roti*.

TAMATARI KABULI CHHOLE

INGREDIENTS :

2 cups large white gram (whole) *(kabuli chhole)*
½ tsp soda-bi-carb
1 tsp salt
½ tsp turmeric powder
½ tsp red chilli powder
1 tsp coriander powder
1 tsp *garam masala* (freshly ground)
1 onion
2 red tomatoes (medium-sized)
3-4 green chillies
1 tbsp green coriander (finely chopped)
1 tbsp refined oil
2 cloves
1" stick cinnamon

METHOD :

1. Clean, wash and soak the gram in double the water and ½ tsp salt for about 3-4 hours.
2. Now add salt and pressure cook (do not strain the soak-in water) for 20-30 mts or till done.
3. Puree the tomatoes, finely chop the onions and cross-slit green chillies.
4. Heat oil in a heavy bottomed pan, add cloves and cinnamon and allow to crackle.
5. Stir-fry the onions till pink and add all the dry spices.
6. Add tomato puree and stir-fry till the mixture leaves oil.
7. Add the boiled gram along with water and cook for 5-6 mts.
8. Adjust water (consistency) to liking, bring to a boil and simmer for 5-6 mts.
9. Serve hot garnished with chillies and coriander.
10. You can enjoy the delicious *chhole* with rice or *puri* or *kulchas*.

SHOARWEDAAR KALE CHANE

INGREDIENTS :

1½ cups whole Bengal gram (*kale chane*)
2 tbsp onion paste
1 tbsp ginger-garlic paste
½ cup tomato pulp
1 tsp salt
¼ tsp turmeric powder
½ tsp red chilli powder
2 tsp coriander powder
½ tsp *garam masala* (freshly ground)
2 large potatoes (quartered)
1 tbsp green coriander (finely chopped)
1 tbsp oil
3-4 bay leaf

METHOD :

1. Wash and soak the gram overnight in saline water.
2. Next morning pressure cook the soaked gram for 30 mts.
3. Heat oil, add bay leaf to it and allow to crackle.
4. Add onion and ginger-garlic pastes to it and stir-fry till pink.
5. Soak the spices in ¼ cup of water for 5-10 mts, add to the onions and stir-fry so as to remove the rawness of the spices.
6. When done add tomato pulp to it and stir and rub against the pan floor with a ladle.
7. When the tomatoes are done add potatoes and keep stirring till the aroma arises. Add boiled gram, mix well and pressure cook for another 10 mts.
8. Sprinkle chopped coriander and *garam masala* and serve hot with steamed rice or *roti*.

① Faloan ka Raita—p. 37
② Dahi ki Gujhia—p. 38

KALE CHANE KHILWAN

INGREDIENTS :

2 cups whole Bengal gram *(kale chane)*
1 tsp cummin seeds
1½ tsp salt
1 tsp *garam masala*
1 tsp red chilli powder
1 tsp dried mango *(amchoor)* powder
½ cup cottage chccsc *(paneer)* (diced)
4 green chillies (finely chopped)
1 tbsp green coriander (finely chopped)
2 onions (finely chopped)
1 tbsp pure *ghee* or refined oil

METHOD :

1. Clean, wash and soak the gram for four hours.
2. Add 2 cups of water and salt to it and pressure cook for 20 mts or till done. Evaporate the access water.
3. Heat *ghee* in a *karahi,* add cummin seeds to it and stir-fry.
4. Add *garam masala*, dried mango *(amchoor)* powder and red chilli powder and stir.
5. Add boiled gram, cottage cheese and onions and stir-fry till done.
6. Serve hot garnished with chopped chillies and coriander.

This hot and sour dish can be enjoyed with both *parantha* and toast.

If the left-over water is too much, strain it and use it as soup and stock.

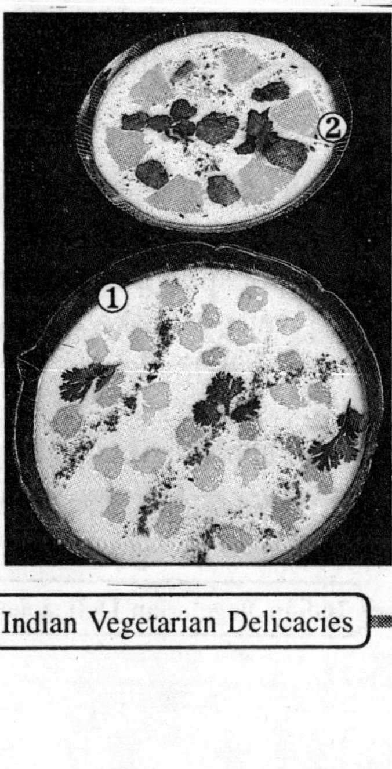

① Jelly Crystal Raita—p. 39
② Ping-Pong Raita—p. 40

SHAHI MEWA KARHI

INGREDIENTS :

For *karhi* :

1½ cups gram flour *(besan)*
½ litre *chhach* or sour curd
¾ tsp turmeric powder
¾ tsp red chilli powder
1½ tsp salt
½ tsp mustard seeds
8-10 curry leaves
½ tbsp *panchforan* (combination of five spices) (cummin seeds, cloves, thyme, asafoetida and fenugreek seeds)
1½ tbsp pure *ghee* or oil
2 dried red chillies

For *pakoris* :

1 cup combined dry fruits (cashews, almonds, *chiraunji,* melon seeds, raisins, dried dates and dried apricots)
a pinch of soda-bi-carb
1 cup *besan*
½ tsp salt
1 cup puffed lotus seeds *(makhanas)* (fried)

METHOD :

To make *karhi* :

1. Take the *chhach* or curd in a large bowl and whisk in flour, salt, red chilli powder and turmeric powder. Take care that lumps of flour do not form.
2. Heat one tbsp oil in a *karahi* or a heavy-bottomed pan, add red chillies and *panchforan* to it and allow to crackle.
3. Add the flour-curd mixture to the crackling spices and keep stirring so that neither lumps form nor does the flour stick to the bottom.
4. Let the *karhi* boil and thicken to desired texture. Drop a *kalchhi* or ladle in it so that the *karhi* keeps boiling but does not spill over.

To make *pakori* :

1. Sieve the flour, soda and salt together.
2. Seed and chop the dates and apricots and add all the dry fruits to the flour.
3. Make a thick batter with a little water taking care that no lump forms.
4. Heat oil in a frying pan, put spoonfuls of batter and fry till golden brown to make *mewa-pakoris*. When the *karhi* has thickened, add *pakoris* and fried *makhanas* to it.
5. Heat the left over *ghee*, add mustard and curry leaves to it and allow to crackle. Use the crackling spices to temper the *karhi.*

HARA-BHARA LOBHIYA

INGREDIENTS :

1½ cup black eye beans *(lobhiya)*
3 cup spinach (blanched and pureed)
1 tbsp onion paste
1½ tbsp ginger-garlic paste
2 tomatoes (pureed)
¾ tsp salt
½ tsp turmeric powder
½ tsp red chilli powder
2 tsp coriander powder
½ tsp *garam masala* (freshly ground)
1 tbsp cream or *malai* (whisked)
1 tbsp green coriander (finely chopped)
1 tbsp oil
3-4 green chillies (finely chopped)

METHOD :

1. Clean and wash the beans and pressure cook in salted water till done.
2. Heat oil in a pressure cooker, add onion and ginger-garlic paste and stir-fry till pink.
3. Soak all the spices except *garam masala* in ¼ cup of water for 5-10 mts and add to the cooking onions. Stir-fry till the aroma rises.
4. Stir in spinach and tomato purees and let it simmer for a few mts stirring in-between.
5. Add the boiled beans, cover and pressure cook for further 10 mts.
6. Sprinkle *garam masala*, green chillies and chopped coriander on top. Garnish with whisked *malai*/cream and serve the deliciously thick *Hara-Bhara Lobhiya* with *naan* or *tandoori roti*.

RAJMA SPECIAL

INGREDIENTS :

2 cups kidney beans *(rajma)*
1 cup cream *(malai)*
2 onions (halved and sliced)
1 tbsp ginger-garlic paste
1 cup tomato puree
1 tsp salt
½ tsp turmeric powder
1 tsp red chilli powder
2 tsp coriander powder
4 eggs (boiled)
4 potatoes (boiled, poked with a fork and cubed)
1 tbsp green coriander (finely chopped)
1½ tbsp oil
2-3 green chillies (finely chopped)

METHOD :

1. Wash and soak the beans overnight.
2. Next morning add salt and pressure cook till done.
3. Heat oil in a pan and stir-fry the onions till pink.
4. Add cream *(malai)* and stir-fry till it leaves fat.
5. Stir-in ginger-garlic pastes, add all the spices and ¼ cup water and stir-fry.
6. Stir-in tomato puree and when the mixture leaves fat add boiled beans, potatoes and chopped green chillies and pressure cook for 5-7 mts.
7. Serve hot garnished with *malai*, coriander and quartered or sliced eggs.

You can avoid potatoes if using eggs and vice-versa.

CHHOLE KHAS

INGREDIENTS :

1 cup (100 grams) whole white gram *(kabuli chhole)*
1 tsp tea leaves
1 tsp salt
2 tsp *kala chaat masala*
1 tsp dried mango *(amchoor)* powder
5 cloves
5 cardamoms
5 black cardamoms
1" stick cinnamon
8-10 bay leaves
15-20 black pepper
2 lemons
2 onions (optional)
1 tbsp green coriander (finely chopped)
2 potatoes (medium-sized)
2 red tomatoes (medium-sized)
5-6 green chillies
½ tsp soda-bi-carb
½ cup refined oil

METHOD :

1. Wash and soak the gram overnight or at-least 5-6 hours in 4 cups of water and salt.
2. Transfer the soaked gram (do not strain) to a pressure cooker and add another cup of water if required.
3. Add soda, tea leaves (tied in a fine muslin) and pressure cook for 20-30 mts.
4. After the first whistle give the cooker a shake so as to spread the colour imparted by tea leaves.
5. Meanwhile, peel and finely chop onions, half and slice tomatoes, chop chillies lengthwise and make potato fingers.
6. In a *karahi*, heat refined oil and fry potato fingers till golden brown.
7. Add all the whole spices to the remaining oil and allow to crackle.
8. Add *kala masala* and mango powder and stir. Now add the boiled gram and cook till done.
9. When ready add chopped onions, tomatoes, chillies and half the coriander, cover and let it stay for 5-6 mts and turn off the heat.
10. Serve steaming hot garnished with potato fingers and chopped coriander.

If *kala masala* is not available then any of the branded *chana masalas* can be used.

DAL MAKHANI

INGREDIENTS :

1½ cups black gram *(urad dal)*
⅓ cup kidney beans *(rajma)*
1 onion (finely chopped)
1" piece of ginger (crushed)
2 cloves of garlic (crushed)
1 tsp salt
½ tsp turmeric powder
½ tsp red chilli powder
a pinch of asafoetida
1 tomato (finely chopped)
½ cup cream or white butter
1 tbsp pure *ghee*
2 red chillies (dried)
2-3 green chillies (finely chopped)

METHOD :

1. Wash, clean and soak the beans and grams in 3 cups of water for 3-4 hours.
2. Add salt, turmeric powder, red chilli powder, ginger and 3 cups of water and pressure cook for 30 mts.
3. Heat *ghee* in a pan and stir-fry onions till pink.
4. Add garlic and dried chillies and stir-fry.
5. Stir in chopped tomatoes, add boiled pulses and allow to boil.
6. Remove from heat and serve the delicious *Dal Makhani* topped with cream or white butter.

PANCHRATNI DAL

INGREDIENTS :

1 cup mixed pulses (include equal parts of lentil *(saboot masoor),* black gram *(urad dal),* green gram *(moong dal),* red gram *(arhar dal)* and Bengal gram *(chana dal)* (washed and skinned))
½ tsp coriander seeds
2 dried red chillies
1 tsp salt
½ tsp turmeric powder
½ tsp red chilli powder
a pinch of asafoetida
¼ tsp cummin seeds
1 tbsp pure *ghee* or butter

METHOD :

1. Clean, wash and soak the pulses for about an hour.
2. Wash and strain the soaked pulses and transfer to a pressure cooker. Add salt, turmeric powder, red chilli powder and 3 cups of water and pressure cook for 30-40 mts.
3. Check if *dal* is done and if necessary pressure cook for another 5 mts.
4. To prepare tempering, heat *ghee* in a tempering pan, add cummin seeds, coriander seeds, dried red chillies and asafoetida and allow to crackle.
5. Temper *dal* with the tempering and cover it for 2-3 mts. Serve hot.

MALKA MASOOR KI DAL

INGREDIENTS :

1 cup lentil *(malka masoor)* (washed and skinned)
1 tsp salt
¼ tsp red chilli powder
¼ tsp turmeric powder
¼ tsp cummin seeds
1 dried red chilli
1 tbsp pure *ghee*
2 cloves of garlic (finely chopped) (optional)
1 onion (finely chopped) (optional)

METHOD :

1. Clean, wash and soak lentil for 15-20 mts.
2. Wash, strain and pressure cook (for 8 mts) along with 4 cups of water, salt, turmeric powder and red chilli powder.
3. Heat *ghee* in a pan and stir-fry chopped onion and garlic to golden.
4. Stir in cummin seeds and dried red chillies.
5. Add boiled lentil, bring to a boil and remove from heat.
6. Serve piping hot with rice or *roti*.

SABZIAN

.(Main coarse preparations)

CHATPATE AALOO LIPATWAAN

INGREDIENTS :

500 grams potatoes
2 large tomatoes
4 green chillies (finely chopped)
a pinch of asafoetida
¼ tsp cummin seeds
1 tsp salt
1 tsp red chilli powder
¼ tsp turmeric powder
2 tsp coriander powder
1 tbsp green coriander (finely chopped)
1 tbsp oil

METHOD :

1. Boil, peel and mash the potatoes.
2. Heat oil, add asafoetida and cummin seeds and allow to crackle.
3. Mix all the spices (except *garam masala*) with ¼ cup of water, add to the crackling mixture and stir-fry.
4. Chop tomatoes and stir-fry. Stir-in chopped chillies.
5. Add mashed potatoes.
6. Add 3 cups of water and cook covered till done, thicken and remove from heat.
7. Sprinkle coriander and *garam masala* and serve with *paranthas* or *kachauris*.

BHARWAAN LAUKI

INGREDIENTS :

1 medium white gourd *(lauki)* (round)
6 large onions (halved and sliced)
2 large tomatoes (pureed)
3 tbsp gram flour *(besan)* (dry roasted)
1½ tsp salt
1½ tsp red chilli powder
½ tsp turmeric powder
2 tsp coriander powder
1 tsp *garam masala* powder
2-3 bay leaf
2 tbsp oil

METHOD :

1. Peel gourd, slice off the top and scoop out the pulp (seeds, etc) leaving a thick outside edge. Finely chop the pulp and keep aside.
2. Heat oil, add sliced onions and stir-fry till pink.
3. Add spices (except *garam masala*), sprinkle a little water and cook till done.
4. Divide the fried *masala* into two parts and to one add the chopped gourd pulp, stir-fry and cook covered till done.
5. Strain cooked pulp and save oil.
6. Add roasted flour to the cooked pulp and mix well to prepare the stuffing.
7. Stuff gourd with the stuffing.
8. Heat the other part of the fried *masala* and add tomato puree. When the gravy starts simmering keep the stuffed gourd in the centre and pressure cook till done.
9. Sprinkle *garam masala* and serve the *Bharwaan Lauki* as a whole or in slices.

BHINDI MASALA FRY

INGREDIENTS :

250 grams okra *(bhindi)*
½ tsp salt
½ tsp dried mango *(amchoor)* powder
½ tsp red chilli powder
½ tsp coriander powder
¼ tsp *garam masala* powder
oil for frying

METHOD :

1. Clean and wash the okra, chop off the ends and slit them lengthwise.
2. Heat oil or *ghee* in a *karahi*, stir-fry the okra and strain out.
3. Heat half a tsp of left over *ghee* or oil, add all the spices and stir-fry till done.
4. Add fried okra and stir-fry till done.
5. *Bhindi Masala Fry* is ready to be served or taken.

This dish does not get spoiled for a long period and so can be carried on journey.

ZIMIKAND BHUNWAAN

INGREDIENTS :

500 grams yam *(zimikand)* (peeled and cubed)
4 large onions (halved and finely sliced)
8-10 curry leaves
½ tsp mustard seeds
1 tsp salt
1 tsp dried mango *(amchoor)* powder
1 tsp red chilli powder
1 tsp *garam masala* powder
2 tbsp oil
2 dried red chillies

METHOD :

1. Wash chopped yam and steam-cook in 1½ cup of water, salt and mango powder to just tender.
2. Heat oil, crackle curry leaves and mustard and add dried red chillies.
3. Add chopped onions when the chillies begin to crackle and stir-fry till done.
4. Add steamed yam along with water, sprinkle red chilli powder and *garam masala* powder, mix well and cook covered till all the water has evaporated.
5. Serve steaming hot with *paranthas*.

SHAHI GOBHI MUSSALAM

INGREDIENTS :

1 cauliflower (large but short)
2½ cups tomato puree
1 cup *khoya* (milk condensed to dry)
1 tbsp green coriander (finely chopped)
1½ tsp salt
½ tsp turmeric powder
1 tsp red chilli powder
1 tsp *garam masala* powder
3-4 bay leaf
1½ tbsp *garam masala* (whole)
2 tbsp ginger paste
2 tbsp almonds and cashew-nut paste
1 cup oil

METHOD :

1. Chop off the leaves and stem taking care that the flower is not damaged and wash the cauliflower thoroughly in running water. Shake off excess water and keep in air to dry out the surface water.
2. Combine *khoya* and dry fruits and keep aside.
3. Heat oil and fry entire flower by turning and tumbling.
4. Remove on a tilted tray or plate so that the oil is drained.
5. Reheat the strained oil, add bay leaf and whole *garam masala* and allow to crackle.
6. Add ginger paste and turmeric and stir-fry. Add red chilli powder and tomato puree and bring to a boil.
7. Add cauliflower and roll it over and over to cook it till tender.
8. Remove to a *karahi*, flower side up, and mount and fill the *khoya* mixture into and around the flower.
9. Add gravy and cover with an inverted *karahi*.
10. Cook covered until the aroma of the cooking *khoya* arises.
11. Put the whole flower to the centre of a serving platter and surround with the gravy.
12. Sprinkle chopped coriander on top and serve steaming.

SABZI PAKORA CURRY

INGREDIENTS :

2 cups mixed seasonal vegetables (cauliflower, capsicum, beans, onions, cabbage, etc) and cottage cheese *(paneer)* (finely chopped)
1 cup cornflour
1 tsp ginger-garlic paste
1¼ tsp salt
1 tsp black pepper (freshly ground)
¼ tsp mono-sodium glutamate (MSG)
1 tbsp vinegar
1 tbsp soya-sauce
2½ cup mixed vegetable stock
oil for frying

METHOD :

1. Dissolve a tbsp of cornflour in a little water and keep aside.
2. Add half the salt and pepper to the rest of it and make a thick paste taking care that no lumps are formed.
3. Add chopped vegetables and deep fry spoonfuls of it in hot oil to make golden brown *pakoras*.
4. Remove *pakoras* on kitchen or brown paper and leave only 2 tbsp of oil in the *karahi*.
5. Add ginger-garlic paste to hot oil and stir-fry to pink.
6. Stir in stock, soya sauce, salt, pepper and MSG and bring to a boil.
7. Turn down the flame to low, add the cornflour mixture while stirring and simmer till thick.
8. Stir in the fried *pakoras* and mix with a gentle hand.
9. Serve steaming with *naan* or *roti*.

GATTE KI SABZI

INGREDIENTS :

2 cups gram flour *(besan)*
3 medium-sized onions
½" piece of ginger (ground)
1½ tsp salt
1½ tsp red chilli powder
2 tsp coriander powder
½ tsp turmeric powder
1 tsp *garam masala* powder
1 tbsp green coriander (finely chopped)
2 dried red chillies
2 black cardamoms
oil for frying

METHOD :

1. Sieve gram flour and add ½ tsp salt and ½ tsp red chilli powder.
2. Dice/finely chop one onion, add to gram flour and knead to small cucumber shaped logs using water.
3. Steam the logs in boiling water and divide into slices when done and a bit hard/stiff. Save the left over water.
4. Heat oil and fry the slices to pink to make *gattas*.
5. Grind 2 onions along with ginger and keep aside.
6. Heat 2 tbsp of oil, add black cardamoms and dried chillies and allow to crackle.
7. Add onion-ginger paste and stir-fry till pink. Add all the spices except *garam masala*, add ½ cup water and cook till done.
8. Add fried *gattas* and stir-fry. Add water used to boil the *gattas* and add more to obtain the desired amount of gravy.
9. Bring to a boil and then pressure cook for 10 mts or till done.
10. Sprinkle *garam masala* on top and garnish with chopped coriander. Serve hot with *paranthas*.

DUM AALOO

INGREDIENTS :

½ kg potatoes (small variety) (boiled and peeled)
1 cup sour curd
¼ cup onion-ginger-garlic paste
3-4 green chillies (finely chopped)
½ tsp turmeric powder
1 tsp salt
1 tbsp green coriander (finely chopped)
¼ tsp cummin seeds
1 tbsp whole *garam masala* (cloves, cinnamon and peppercorns)
2 tomatoes (pureed)
oil (to requirement)

METHOD :

1. Heat oil, fry all the potatoes and keep aside.
2. To hot oil add whole *garam masala* and cummin seeds and allow to crackle.
3. Add onion mixture and stir-fry till reddish brown.
4. Add turmeric powder, salt and tomato puree and stir-fry. Stir in the curd and fry till the mixture leaves oil.
5. Add a cup of water and bring the curry to a boil.
6. Add fried potatoes and cook covered till thick and done.
7. Sprinkle coriander and enjoy hot with *roti* or *parantha*.

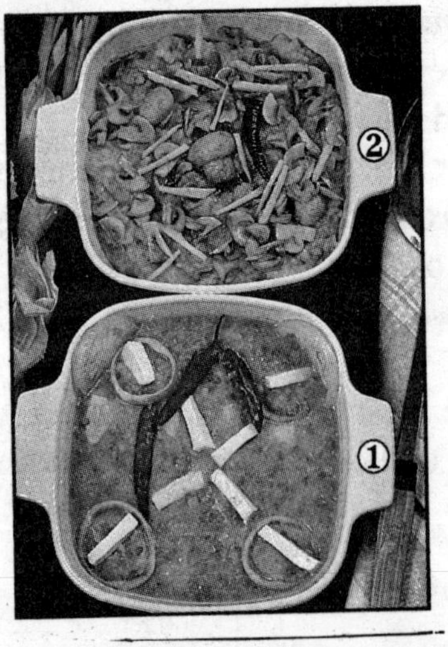

① Saabut Moong Paneeri—p. 46
② Urad Mushroom—p. 47

KELE KI MARGUL CURRY

INGREDIENTS :

3 raw green bananas
1 cup gram flour *(besan)*
2 onions (medium-sized, chopped)
½" piece of ginger (chopped)
2-3 cloves of garlic (ground along with onions and ginger)
1½ tsp salt
½ tsp turmeric powder
1½ tsp red chilli powder
1½ tsp coriander powder
½ tsp dried mango *(amchoor)* powder
¼ tsp thyme seeds
oil for frying

METHOD :

1. Peel bananas, finely slice them lengthwise and soak them in water.
2. Combine flour, ½ tsp salt, ½ tsp red chilli powder and dried mango *(amchoor)* powder and make a thick batter with water.
3. Heat *ghee* or oil. Dip soaked banana slices in the batter and deep fry to golden brown on low flame to make *kela margul*.
4. Leave only a tbsp of oil in the *karahi* and add the onion-garlic paste to hot oil.
5. Stir-fry till golden, add all the spices (except *garam masala*) and ½ cup of water and cook till done.
6. When the fat leaves oil, add 7-8 cups of water and let it boil.
7. Add fried marguls when the gravy is done and simmer on low flame for 15-20 mts.
8. Serve hot garnished with *garam masala* powder, chopped coriander, etc.

① Shahi Mewa Karhi—p. 56
② Hara-Bhara Lobhiya—p. 57

MALAI KEBAB

INGREDIENTS :

2 medium potatoes (boiled and grated)
2 slice bread (crust removed)
2½ cups cottage cheese *(paneer)* (crumbled)
½ tsp salt
¼ tsp black pepper (freshly ground)
1 cup *malai* or thick cream
10-12 raisins
10-12 *chiraunji*

For the gravy :

2 medium onions (chopped)
½" piece of ginger (chopped)
3-4 cloves of garlic (ground together with onion and ginger)
3-4 green chillies (chopped)
1 tsp salt
¼ tsp turmeric powder
2 tsp coriander powder
¾ tsp red chilli powder
1 cup tomato puree
½ tsp *garam masala* powder
1 tbsp green coriander (finely chopped)
1 tbsp *malai* or thick cream (whisked)
oil (to requirement)

METHOD :

1. Soak bread, squeeze out excess water, mash and combine with grated potato, crumbled *paneer*, pepper and salt. Knead to make a uniform log.
2. Combine *malai*/cream, raisins and *chiraunji* and keep aside.
3. Divide the log into equal portions. Flatten each portion on moist palm, keep a little *malai*/cream mixture in the centre, carefully reseal the *kebab* and shape as rolls.
4. Heat oil, deep fry all the *kebab* to golden.
5. To make the gravy mix all dry spices (except *garam masala* powder) with ¼ cup of water and keep aside.
6. Heat 2 tbsp oil and stir-fry the ground onion mixture till pink.
7. Add soaked *masala* and stir-fry till done.
8. Add tomato puree and enough water to have the desired amount of gravy and cook till thick.
9. Sprinkle *garam masala* powder.
10. Just before serving, add *kebabs* and sprinkle chopped coriander.
11. Garnish with *malai* and serve the rich *kebabs* piping hot with *roti, puri* or *naan.*

KHADA MASALA DAHI GOBHI

INGREDIENTS :

1 cauliflower *(gobhi)* (medium-sized)
2 potatoes (medium-sized)
4 onions (medium-sized)
4-6 dried red chillies
4-6 bay leaf
2 tomatoes
4-6 black cardamoms
10 pepper corns
3-4 pieces cinnamon
4-5 cloves
2 cups curd
1 tbsp green coriander (finely chopped)
1¼ tsp salt
½ tsp red chilli powder
1½ tsp oil

METHOD :

1. Divide cauliflower into sizeable florets and quarter potatoes, onions and tomatoes.
2. Heat oil, add dried red chillies, bay leaves, pepper corns, cinnamon, cloves and black cardamoms and reduce the flame to low.
3. Add chopped vegetables, remaining spices and curd, cover and cook on medium-low flame for 20 mts.
4. Cook till the vegetables are just done so that they remain crunchy.
5. Remove the cover and evaporate whatever liquid is left.
6. Sprinkle chopped coriander and serve hot with *paranthas*.

BHARWAAN SHIMLA MIRCH

INGREDIENTS :

5-6 medium capsicum (Shimla *mirch*)
½ cup cabbage (shredded)
½ cup french beans (finely chopped)
½ cup carrot (finely diced)
1 medium potato (finely diced)
1 medium onion (finely chopped)
2 green chillies (finely chopped)
½ tsp mustard seeds
8-10 curry leaves
1 tsp salt
½ tsp red chilli powder
½ tsp black pepper (freshly ground)
2 tbsp oil

METHOD :

1. Clean and wash capsicum and slit-off the top along with the seed cluster. Separate the cover and the seed cluster and finely chop the seed cluster. Do not discard the cover.
2. Brush empty capsicums and their cover with oil.
3. Heat the remaining oil. Add curry leaves and mustard and allow to crackle.
4. Add all the chopped vegetables and capsicum seeds and cook on low flame for 5-7 mts or till done.
5. Stir to evaporate the excess water and stuff empty capsicums with the prepared stuffing. Replace the tops to cover.
6. Either bake the stuffed capsicums in a pre-heated oven at 200' for 10-15 mts or secure the covers with thread and shallow fry on all sides till done.
7. Serve hot (thread removed, if used) along with *roti*, etc.

MOONG PAKORI CURRY

INGREDIENTS :

2 cups green gram *(moong dhuli)* (washed, skinned, soaked and ground to paste along with a pinch of asafoetida, ½" piece of ginger and 2-3 green chillies)
¼ cup onion-ginger-garlic paste
3-4 green cardamom
1½ tsp salt
2 tsp coriander powder
1½ tsp red chilli powder
¼ tsp turmeric powder
1 tsp *garam masala* powder
green coriander (finely chopped) as a condiment
oil (to requirement)

METHOD :

1. Add ½ tsp salt and ½ tsp red chilli powder to ground gram *(pitthi)* and whisk.
2. Heat oil and make *pakoris* by frying teaspoonfuls of *pitthi* to golden brown.
3. Leave only 2 tbsp of oil in the *karahi*, heat and add green cardamoms.
4. When the cardamoms begin to crackle, add onion-garlic paste, stir-fry, add all the spices (except *garam masala*) and cook till done.
5. Add 5-7 cups of water and let the curry cook on medium-high flame.
6. Add *pakoris* to the boiling curry and cook till it thickens.
7. Serve hot garnished with *garam masala* powder, chopped coriander, etc. and enjoy with *roti*.

SAFED (WHITE) SAUCE MAIN SABZIAN

INGREDIENTS :

3 cups mixed vegetables (chopped) (capsicum, shelled peas, carrot, cabbage, cottage cheese *(paneer)*, beans and cauliflower)
2 tbsp all purpose flour *(maida)*
1 large onion (chopped)
1 glass milk
½ cup processed cheese (grated)
1¼ tsp salt
1 tsp black pepper (freshly ground)
2 tbsp oil or butter

METHOD :

1. Boil water in a pan, add chopped vegetables to the boiling water, and cook for 2 mts, strain out the vegetables and save water as stock.
2. Heat oil or butter and stir-fry chopped onions to pink. Add flour and again stir-fry to pink.
3. Add stock and keep on stirring so that the lumps do not form.
4. Gradually add milk and continue to stir. Stir-in the grated cheese and bring to a boil.
5. Season with salt and pepper and simmer till thick.
6. Add boiled vegetables and fold in the sauce. Mix well and remove from heat.
7. Enjoy with toasted bread or *paranthas*.

PANEER KOFTA

INGREDIENTS :

500 grams cottage cheese *(paneer)*
15-20 raisins
¾ tsp salt
½ tsp black pepper (freshly ground)
1 tbsp all purpose flour *(maida)*
oil for frying

For gravy :
2 onions (ground) (optional)
½ tbsp ginger-green chilli paste
3-4 green cardamoms
1 tsp salt
½ tsp red chilli powder
2 tsp coriander powder
½ tsp turmeric powder
3 cups tomatoes (pureed)
1 tsp *garam masala* powder
green coriander (finely chopped) as a condiment

METHOD :

1. Combine *paneer*, flour, salt and pepper and mash between your palms till your palms become greasy and you can make small balls of *paneer*-flour mixture.
2. Embed a raisin in each ball, heat oil and deep fry all the balls to golden brown on medium flame to make *koftas*.
3. Leave only 2 tbsp oil in the *karahi* and crackle green cardamoms in hot oil.
4. Add salt and all the other spices (except *garam masala*) and stir-fry. Add ginger-green chilli paste and stir-fry.
5. If using onions, first stir-fry onion and ginger-green chilli paste to pink and then add and stir-fry the spices.
6. Add pureed tomatoes and continue to stir till done. Add water to increase the gravy to desired amount and let the gravy cook and thicken. Remove from heat once done.
7. Before serving add the *koftas* and bring to a boil.
8. Serve hot garnished with *garam masala* powder, chopped coriander and enjoy the delicious *paneer koftas* with *tandoori roti* or *naan*.

LAGAA-LIPTA KATHAL

INGREDIENTS :

500 grams jackfruit *(kathal)* (chopped)
2 large onions (halved and sliced)
2 tsp coriander powder
1 tsp salt
¾ tsp red chilli powder
¼ tsp turmeric powder
1 tsp *garam masala* powder
3 tbsp oil
1 tbsp *malai* or thick cream

METHOD :

1. Heat oil, fry jackfruit pieces till golden brown and strain out.
2. Reheat the left over oil and stir-fry chopped onions till golden.
3. Add salt, ¼ cup of water and all the other spices (except *garam masala*) and stir-fry till done.
4. Add fried jackfruit, mix well and stir-fry.
5. Stir in a cup of water and pressure cook for 5-7 mts.
6. Remove the lid, stir-fry to evaporate excess water and remove from heat.
7. Serve hot topped with whisked *malai* or cream.

SAAG

INGREDIENTS :

3 cups spinach leaves *(paalak ka saag)* (fresh and shredded)
3 cups mustard leaves *(sarson ka saag)* (fresh and shredded)
1 cup Bengal gram leaves *(chane ka saag)* (fresh and shredded)
½ cup radish leave *(mooli ke patte)* (fresh and shredded)
½ tsp asafoetida
2 tbsp whole corn flour *(makki ka atta)* or gram flour *(besan)*
1¼ tsp salt
1 tsp red chilli powder
½ tsp turmeric powder
1" piece of ginger
2 tbsp pure *ghee*
2 dried red chillies
1 tomato (finely chopped)
1 onion (finely chopped)

METHOD :

1. Before chopping the green vegetables clean and wash them thoroughly under running water.
2. Boil shredded vegetables in 3 cups of water along with asafoetida, ginger, salt, turmeric powder and red chilli powder. Cook for further 15 mts.
3. Cool and puree the cooked *saag*.
4. Combine flour with a little water and keep aside.
5. Heat *ghee*, crackle dried red chillies and stir-fry the onions to red.
6. Stir-in the pureed *saag*, add flour paste and simmer for 20-25 mts.
7. Temper the *saag* with 1½-tsp red chilli powder crackled in 2 tbsp of hot pure *ghee*.
8. Enjoy the aromatic *saag* with *makki ki roti* and jaggery.

BHARWAAN TAMATAR

INGREDIENTS :

6 tomatoes (large, red and stiff)
1½ cups curd-cheese *(dahi-paneer)* (2½ cups fresh curd hung in a fine muslin for 7-8 hours)
1 large onion
1 tsp salt
1 tsp black pepper (freshly ground)
1 tbsp oil
1 tbsp green coriander (finely chopped)
3-4 green chillies (chopped)

METHOD :

1. Clean, wash and wipe tomatoes with a clean cloth and slit off the tops (do not discard).
2. Scoop out the pulp and keep tomatoes inverted to drain out any liquid present.
3. Heat oil, stir-fry the onions till transparent, strain out and keep in the strainer for a minute or two.
4. Add oil free onions to the thick and creamy curd cheese and combine with salt, black pepper, green chillies and coriander. Mix with a gentle hand to prepare the stuffing.
5. Stuff the empty tomatoes with the stuffing, replace the tops and brush them with oil.
6. Heat a non-stick frying pan and grease it with the strained out oil.
7. Arrange stuffed tomatoes in the pan, cover and cook on medium flame for 5-7 mts. You can even bake the stuffed tomatoes.
8. Serve the steaming hot stuffed tomatoes arranged on a platter.

MEWA MALAI PAALAK

INGREDIENTS :

3 cups spinach leaves (blanched and pureed)
1½ cups *malai* or thick cream
½ cup almonds, cashew nuts and puffed lotus seeds *(makhanas)* (roasted/deep fried)
1 tbsp lemon juice
1 large onion (finely diced/ chopped)
1½ tbsp all purpose flour *(maida)*
1½ tsp sugar
1 tsp salt
¾ tsp black pepper (freshly ground)
1 tbsp oil or *ghee*

METHOD :

1. Heat *ghee* or oil and stir-fry the onions to pink.
2. Add *malai* (save 1 tbsp for garnishing) and stir-fry.
3. When *malai* leaves *ghee* (fat), add flour and stir-fry to pink.
4. Stir-in spinach puree and mix well.
5. Add salt, sugar, pepper and lemon juice and let the *malai paalak* simmer and thicken.
6. Add dry fruits and garnish with *malai*.
7. Let your guests drool over the rich and delicious *Mewa Malai Paalak*.

BAKED TINDA

INGREDIENTS :

10-12 round gourds *(tinda)*
4 onions (medium-sized)
1½" piece of ginger (ground to a paste)
1½ tsp salt
1½ tsp black pepper (freshly ground)
1 cup button mushroom (finely chopped)
100 grams processed cheese (grated)
4 large tomatoes
½ cup cream
½ tbsp *ghee* or oil

METHOD :

1. Peel the round gourd. Slit off and discard the top. Scoop out pulp from the gourd and poke them with a fork so that the spices go deep into it when cooked.
2. Finely chop or dice the onions and puree the tomatoes. Strain to remove the seeds and skin if any.
3. Heat oil in a pan and stir-fry the onions to pink.
4. Add ginger paste and gourd pulp, stir-in a tsp each of salt and pepper and stir-fry. When the moisture has evaporated add half the mushrooms.
5. Remove from heat when done and cool the stuffing.
6. Stuff the empty gourds with the ready stuffing and arrange in a greased baking (preferably a bake'n'serve) dish.
7. Combine tomato puree, cream, salt, pepper and remaining mushrooms, mix well and uniformly pour over the arranged stuffed gourds.
8. Sprinkle grated cheese on top and bake in a preheated oven at 250' for 20 mts or till the cheese has browned.
9. Serve hot garnished with chopped coriander.

BATHUA KOFTA CURRY

INGREDIENTS :

1 kg *bathua* leaves
2 potatoes (medium-sized)
2 onions (medium-sized)
1" piece of ginger
4 cloves of garlic (ground to paste with onions and ginger)
1½ tsp salt
1 tsp red chilli powder
¾ tsp turmeric powder
½ tsp *garam masala* powder
oil for frying
½ cup tomato puree
2 cloves
½ cup green coriander and green chillies (finely chopped)

METHOD :

1. Clean and wash *bathua* and potatoes and pressure cook in a cup of water till done.
2. Meanwhile, finely chop the tomatoes if using.
3. Once done separate potatoes from *bathua*, peel and mash them.
4. Strain *bathua*, squeeze-out excess water and grind to a paste.
5. Combine *bathua* paste, mashed potatoes, ½ tsp each of salt and chilli powder and a little chopped coriander and chillies and mash together to form a uniform log.
6. Heat oil or *ghee* in a *karahi*.
7. Divide the log into round *koftas* of 1½" diameter and fry them till done in hot oil.
8. Leave only a tbsp of oil in the *karahi*, heat it and crackle cloves.
9. Add the ground mixture and stir-fry till golden. Add all the spices (except *garam masala*), stir-fry, add a little water and cook till done.
10. Stir-in tomato puree and when the *masala* leaves oil add a glass of water and let the gravy cook.
11. After a boil or two add fried *koftas* and simmer on medium-high flame till gravy thickens or is reduced.
12. Serve hot garnished with *garam masala* powder, chopped coriander and green chillies.

SUNHARI ARVI

INGREDIENTS :

½ kg colocasia *(arvi)*
¼ tsp thyme seeds
a pinch of asafoetida
1 tsp salt
½ tsp red chilli powder
½ tsp *garam masala* powder
oil for frying

METHOD :

1. Clean and wash thoroughly colocasia and pressure cook to just done. Remove to cold water immediately.
2. Peel off the skin and finely slice colocasia.
3. Heat oil in a *karahi* and fry colocasia slices to golden.
4. Remove *ghee* from the *karahi* and to the hot *karahi* add a pinch of asafoetida and fried slices and stir well.
5. Add all the spices and stir-fry on low flame for another 5 mts.
6. *Sunhari Arvi* is ready.

PAALAK KOFTA CURRY

INGREDIENTS :

1 kg spinach leaves *(paalak)*
200 grams cottage cheese *(paneer)*
½ cup breadcrumbs
½ tsp salt
½ tsp black pepper (freshly ground)
8-10 cashew nuts for garnishing (optional)
oil for frying

For the curry :

2 onions
1" piece of ginger
4 cloves of garlic (all ground together to a paste) (optional)
4 tomatoes (pureed)
1½ cup curd
1 tsp salt
1 tsp coriander powder
½ tsp red chilli powder
½ tsp turmeric powder
1 tsp *garam masala* powder
2-3 cloves

METHOD :

1. Clean spinach, wash off the grit under running water and pressure cook without any water for 3-4 mts.
2. Cool, strain out spinach and save the stock. Squeeze out the excess stock and save it too.
3. Grind spinach in a grinder or on pestle and mortar to a stiff paste and mash along with breadcrumbs to form a uniform log. Divide it into equal balls of 1½" diameter.
4. Combine *paneer*, salt and pepper and mash to prepare the stuffing.
5. Stuff each *paalak* ball with a little *paneer* stuffing to make round *koftas*.
6. Heat oil and fry *koftas* to pink.
7. Leave only a tbsp or two of oil in the *karahi* and crackle cloves in hot oil.
8. Stir-fry ground onion mixture to golden, add all the spices (except *garam masala*), stir-fry, add ¼ cup of water and cook till done.
9. Stir-in curd, simmer till thick, add tomato puree and cook.
10. Add spinach stock and cook till the gravy turns red. Add fried *koftas* and remove from heat.
11. Serve hot garnished with *garam masala* powder and cashew nuts and enjoy with *rumali roti.*

MIRCH PANEER

INGREDIENTS :

500 grams cottage cheese *(paneer)*
3 large capsicums
2 large onions
2 cups tomato juice
1 tsp ginger-garlic paste
1 tbsp soya sauce
1 tbsp vinegar
1 tbsp chilli sauce
1 cup mix vegetable stock
1 tbsp cornflour
¼ tsp mono-sodium glutamate (MSG)
1 tsp salt
1 tsp black pepper (freshly ground)
3½-4 tbsp oil

METHOD :

1. Cube *paneer*, quarter onions and separate the individual layers/leaves.
2. Chop capsicums to medium-sized pieces.
3. Heat oil, fry *paneer* cubes lightly and strain out.
4. Similarly fry capsicum and set aside.
5. In the remaining hot oil add chopped onions and ginger-garlic paste and stir-fry.
6. Stir-in the stock, tomato juice, sauces, vinegar, salt, pepper and MSG and cook the gravy.
7. Combine the cornflour with ¼ cup of water to make a fine paste and add to the cooking gravy. Let it thicken.
8. Add fried *paneer* and vegetables, mix well, cover and cook for a few mts on low flame.
9. Serve deliciously hot *Mirch Paneer* with *tandoori roti, naan* or toasted bread.

① Mirch Paneer—p. 88
② Palak Kofta Curry—p. 87

MUSHROOM BHUNWAAN

INGREDIENTS :

250 grams whole button mushrooms
4 onions (medium-sized)
1½ tbsp oil
3-4 green chillies
¾ tsp salt
¾ tsp black pepper (freshly ground)
1 small cup shelled peas

METHOD :

1. Clean, wash and slice mushrooms.
2. Peel and halve the onions and finely slice them.
3. Heat oil and stir-fry mushrooms and onions. Take care not to break the mushroom slices.
4. Stir in peas, season with salt and pepper, cover and cook till both mushroom and peas are done.
5. Remove the lid and stir-fry to evaporate water.
6. Stir in chopped chillies and serve steaming hot with *paranthas*.

① Mushroom Bhunwaan—p. 91
② Matar Makhana Curry—p. 92

MATAR MAKHANA CURRY

INGREDIENTS :

250 grams peas (fresh and shelled)
2 cups puffed lotus seeds *(makhana)* (halved)
4 large tomatoes
3 tbsp oil
½ cup cream
8-10 cashew nuts (optional)
4 black cardamoms
4 bay leaf
¼ cup onion-ginger-garlic paste (optional)
1 tsp salt
¼ tsp turmeric powder
¾ tsp red chilli powder
2 tsp coriander powder
1 tsp *garam masala* powder

METHOD :

1. Soak salt and all other spices (except *garam masala*) in a little water.
2. Heat oil, fry cashew nuts and *makhanas* and keep aside.
3. In the leftover hot oil, crackle cardamoms and bay leaf and stir-fry onion mixture (if using) to pink.
4. Add the soaked spices (*masala*) and stir-fry till done.
5. Puree the tomatoes, add to the cooking *masala* and continue stirring till done.
6. Stir-in peas, fried *makhanas* and enough water for the desired amount of gravy and pressure cook till thick and done.
7. Remove the lid and cook uncovered. Add the cream and remove from heat once it has boiled.
8. Sprinkle *garam masala* on top and serve hot garnished with fried cashew nuts.

Enjoy with hot steaming *puris*.

BUTTER PANEER

INGREDIENTS :

500 grams cottage cheese *(paneer)*
8-10 tomatoes (juice)
150 grams butter
1 tsp salt
1 tsp black pepper (freshly ground)
½ tbsp sugar
1 lemon (juice)
1 cup cream
1 tbsp green coriander (finely chopped)
2 onions (medium-sized, finely chopped)
fried mixed dry fruits for garnishing (optional)

METHOD :

1. Add sugar, salt, pepper, cream and a tbsp of butter to tomato juice and bring to a boil.
2. Reduce the flame to low and simmer for 5-7 mts. Remove from heat.
3. Cube *paneer*, heat a tbsp of oil, lightly fry the cubed *paneer* and strain out.
4. Add remaining butter to the hot butter and stir-fry chopped onions to translucent.
5. Stir in tomato sauce and fried *paneer* cubes and cook till thick.
6. Garnish with dry fruits and chopped coriander and enjoy with *naan*, *kulchas* and salad.

KHOYE KE KEBAB

INGREDIENTS :

250 grams *khoya* (milk condensed to semi-dry)
2 tbsp all purpose flour *(maida)*
a pinch of soda-bi-carb
¼ tsp salt
¼ tsp black pepper (freshly ground)
8-10 raisins
½ tbsp green cardamoms (powdered)

For gravy :
3-4 green cardamoms (powdered)
2 onions (ground to paste) (optional)
1" piece of ginger
3-4 cloves of garlic (crushed) (optional)
1 cup curd
1 cup tomato juice
1 tbsp green coriander (finely chopped)
1 tsp *garam masala* powder
½ tsp salt
¼ tsp turmeric powder
2 tsp coriander powder
oil (to requirement)

METHOD :

1. Crumble *khoya* and combine with salt, soda, flour and pepper. Mash till you can form balls.
2. Divide it into equal (fistfuls) portions and embed a little cardamom and a raisin in the centre of each.
3. Heat oil and fry *kebabs* one or two at a time till golden brown in colour.
4. To make the curry, crackle cardamom powder in 2 tbsp of hot oil.
5. Add onions, ginger and garlic pastes and stir-fry till pink. Add dry spices and cook in ¼ cup of water to remove rawness of the spices.
6. Add curd and tomato juice and stir-fry. Add water to adjust the consistency or quantity and let the gravy cook. Stir in *garam masala* powder and remove from heat.
7. Arrange the *kebabs* in a large shallow serving bowl and pour curry evenly on top.
8. Serve garnished with coriander and enjoy it with *puris* or *paranthas*.

KHATTA-MEETHA KASHIFAL

INGREDIENTS :

250 grams pumpkin *(kashifal)*
1 tsp sugar
¾ tsp salt
¼ tsp turmeric powder
1 tsp coriander powder
¾ tsp red chilli powder
1 tsp dried mango *(amchoor)* powder
2 large onions (optional)
3-4 green chillies (coarsely chopped)
¾ tsp *garam masala* powder
¼ tsp fenugreek seeds
a pinch of asafoetida
½ tbsp oil
1 dried red chilli

METHOD :

1. Clean, wash and chop the pumpkin (do not peel).
2. Halve the onions and finely slice them.
3. Heat oil, crackle dried chilli and add asafoetida and fenugreek seeds.
4. When these begin to crackle, add salt and all other spices (except *garam masala*), add a little water and stir-fry till done.
5. Add chopped vegetables and stir-fry. Add enough water to make the pumpkin tender, cover and cook till done.
6. Add sugar and *garam masala* powder and stir-fry to evaporate the excess water.
7. Serve hot with *berhvee* or *puri*.

BESANI KARELE

INGREDIENTS :

250 grams bitter gourd *(karela)* (washed and finely sliced)
½ cup gram flour *(besan)*
1 onion (medium-sized, finely chopped and washed) or, ¼ tsp cummin seeds
¼ tsp turmeric powder
¾ tsp coriander powder
¼ tsp red chilli powder
¼ tsp *garam masala* powder
2½ tsp salt
1 tbsp *ghee* or oil

METHOD :

1. Sprinkle 1½ tbsp salt on the sliced gourd, mix well and keep aside for 3-4 hours.
2. Dry roast the gram flour on a hot griddle.
3. Heat oil or *ghee* in a heavy-bottomed pan and stir-fry washed onions to golden or crackle the cummin seeds (whichever using).
4. Add rest of the spices and a little water and stir-fry till done.
5. Thoroughly wash the salted gourd slices under running water.
6. When the cooking *masala* leaves oil, add washed *karelas*, stir-fry a bit, add a cup of water and cook on medium flame.
7. When the gourd is done and excess moisture begins to evaporate, add roasted flour and stir-fry till done.
8. *Besani Karele* is ready to be served on the table or get packed up for a picnic or trip.

PAALAK PANEER

INGREDIENTS :

100 grams cottage cheese *(paneer)*
500 grams spinach leaves (blanched and pureed)
½ tsp salt
1 tsp coriander powder
¼ tsp red chilli powder
¼ tsp *garam masala* powder
¼ tsp turmeric powder
1 onion (medium-sized, finely chopped)
1" piece of ginger
2 cloves of garlic
1 tbsp pure *ghee* or oil
2 tomatoes (medium-sized)

METHOD :

1. Cut *paneer* into large and long cubes.
2. Peel and grind the ginger and garlic to make a paste. Finely chop tomatoes.
3. Heat oil in a non-stick frying pan, stir-fry the onions to golden brown and add salt and all other spices (except *garam masala*).
4. Add a little water and stir-fry till the rawness of the spices is removed.
5. When the *masala* starts leaving oil, add tomatoes and stir-fry till done.
6. Add pureed spinach and let it cook, stirring in between.
7. When the spinach leaves oil add *paneer* and a cup of water and let it simmer on low flame for 5-7 mts.
8. Sprinkle *garam masala* on top and serve piping hot.

KARARI PATTAGOBHI

INGREDIENTS :

250 grams cabbage
100 grams shelled peas or mushrooms or capsicum (julienne), potatoes (chopped with their skins)
½ tsp salt
½ tsp black pepper (freshly ground)
¼ tsp red chilli powder
¼ tsp cummin seeds
1 tbsp oil

METHOD :

1. Shred cabbage as fine as possible.
2. Heat oil in a non-stick pan.
3. Add cummin seeds and allow to crackle.
4. Add chopped vegetable and stir-fry.
5. Add all the spices and mix well.
6. When just done add the shredded cabbage and stir-fry.

The crispy *Karari Pattagobhi* is ready.

ROTI-CHAWAL-PULAO

(Grain preparations)

MAKKI KI ROTI

INGREDIENTS :

1 cup whole corn flour *(makki ka atta)*
¼ tsp salt
¼ tsp red chilli powder
1 tbsp whole wheat flour
1 onion (finely chopped) (optional)
pure *ghee*

METHOD :

1. Sift corn and wheat flour together.
2. Add salt, red chilli powder and onions and knead using water.
3. Divide into four parts and make balls.
4. Press each ball with moistened hands or roll out using a rolling pin.
5. Make *chapatis* on a preheated griddle (medium flame) to golden brown.
6. Brush with *ghee* and serve steaming hot with *sarson ka saag* or *urad chane ki dal.*

LATCHAA PARANTHA

INGREDIENTS :

2 cups whole wheat flour
½ tsp salt
¼ tsp thyme seeds
¼ tsp aniseeds (coarsely ground)
1 tbsp pure *ghee* or refined oil
ghee or oil for frying
ghee or butter for serving

METHOD :

1. Sieve flour and combine with thyme seeds, aniseeds, salt and 1 tbsp *ghee*.
2. Add water and knead a little stiff dough.
3. Divide it into three equal dough balls.
4. Take one and roll it out on the clean platform into an 8" square sheet.
5. Line the sheet with *ghee* or oil and fold upwards giving plates with your thumb so that you have a thick strip (2½" by 8") with ridges.
6. Grease your palms and fold this strip lengthwise (along the length of the ridges) to form a thick disc.
7. Roll it out like a *parantha* and fry both sides to golden brown on a preheated griddle. The ridges of the *parantha* will swell out making it look like *latchaa*.

Serve steaming hot with curd, pickle or a main coarse dish.

LUCHAI (MAIDA KI PURI)

INGREDIENTS :

500 grams refined flour *(maida)*
¾ tsp salt
2¼ tbsp *ghee*
oil for frying
a pinch of soda-bi-carb
a pinch of sugar (powdered)

METHOD :

1. Strain flour, make a mound and make a well in the centre.
2. Add salt, soda, *ghee* and sugar in the well and knead with water.
3. Divide into equal small portions and roll out small *luchais* using a rolling pin.
4. Heat oil and deep fry white puffed *luchais.*
5. Enjoy hot-steaming *luchais* with *aaloo ki sabzi.*

BERHVEE

INGREDIENTS :

2 cups whole wheat flour
1 tsp salt
½ cup black gram (washed and skinned) *(urad dhuli dal)*
½" piece of ginger
3-4 green chillies
a pinch of asafoetida
¼ tsp aniseeds
oil or *ghee* for frying

METHOD :

1. Clean, wash and soak *dal* for half an hour.
2. Add salt to the flour and knead using water.
3. Strain soaked *dal* and grind to a thick paste *(pitthi)* along with chopped green chillies, chopped ginger, asafoetida and aniseeds.
4. Heat a tsp of *ghee* and stir-fry the *pitthi* till dry and hard.
5. Divide dough into small equal balls.
6. Create a depression in the centre of each ball, spoon ¼ tsp *pitthi*, seal and make ball again. Stack-up stuffed dough balls from rest of the dough.
7. Heat oil in a *karahi*.
8. Roll out each ball carefully so as to avoid exposing the *pitthi* and deep fry small *berhvees* to red and crisp. Applying slight pressure with the strainer while frying makes the *berhvees* swell out.

Serve steaming with fenugreek *chutney* or hot and sour potatoes.

BHATURE

INGREDIENTS :

5 cups all purpose flour
1 tsp salt
1 tsp sugar
1 tsp soda-bi-carb
1 cup sour curd
½ cup *ghee* or oil
oil for frying
For filling (mashed cottage cheese, mashed boiled potato, ground green chillies and green coriander)
1½ tsp onion seeds (optional)

METHOD :

1. Combine flour, salt and soda and sift.
2. Make a mound of the sifted flour, create a pit in the centre with your hands and fill it with sugar, curd and ½ cup *ghee* or oil.
3. Knead with lukewarm water to a soft dough, transfer to a deep large pan, cover with moistened muslin and let the dough rise (ferment) for eight hours.
4. When the dough has risen and doubled in quantity, divide it into equal fistfuls portions.
5. Stuff and seal each ball with the filling if using.
6. Grease your palms and spread out each *bhatura* by applying pressure with your palms. If there is problem, grease a plastic wrap, fold lengthwise, keep a dough ball between its folds and roll out *bhatura* using a rolling pin.
7. Sprinkle a few onion seeds on each *bhatura* and deep fry till golden on both sides. Applying pressure with the strainer while frying makes the *bhaturas* swell out.
8. Serve steaming hot with *chatpate chhole.*

PURI

INGREDIENTS :

2½ cups whole wheat flour
¼ tsp salt (optional)
2 tbsp *ghee* or oil
oil for frying

METHOD :

1. Sift flour and salt together.
2. Knead a slightly hard dough using water.
3. Sprinkle a tbsp of oil or *ghee* and knead again so that the dough absorbs the oil.
4. Apply oil in your hands and divide the dough into equal balls.
5. Grease the rolling board or platform and the rolling pin and roll out small circular or elliptical *puris*.
6. Heat oil or *ghee* in a *karahi* and fry the *puris* on both sides till golden pink and puffed as a ball.

Serve and enjoy with *chhole*, *raita* or pickle.

KHAMIRI ROTI

INGREDIENTS :

300 grams all purpose flour
¼ cup milk
½ tbsp sugar (powdered)
1 tsp salt
¼ cup oil
oil for frying

METHOD :

1. Sieve the flour and keep 3 tbsp aside. To the rest of it add sugar and salt and knead to a soft dough using milk.
2. Cover with a moist cloth and let it ferment for 8-10 hours.
3. Sprinkle rest of the flour and ¼ cup oil on it and knead to soft. Use water if necessary.
4. Grease the rolling pin and board and roll out *khamiri rotis*.
5. Fry the *rotis* and enjoy with vegetarian and non-vegetarian delicacies (dry or with gravy).

NAAN

INGREDIENTS :

2 cups all purpose flour *(maida)*
½ cup sour curd
¼ cup milk
1 tsp baking powder
a pinch soda-bi-carb
2 tsp *ghee* or oil
½ tsp salt
1 tbsp onion seeds
1 tbsp green coriander (finely chopped)

METHOD :

1. Combine flour, salt, soda and baking powder and sieve.
2. Add curd and milk and knead to a soft dough. Cover and keep aside for a few mts.
3. Knead again, cover with a moist cloth and let it ferment for 3-4 hours.
4. Divide the dough into 8-10 equal balls. Roll them to form round, elliptical or triangular *naans.*
5. Sprinkle onion seeds on each and apply slight pressure with fingers to embed them.
6. Bake to golden in an oven or *tandoor*.
7. Brush butter on top and enjoy with both non-vegetarian and vegetarian delicacies.

In case neither oven nor *tandoor* is available moisten the *naan* on one side and stick to a hot griddle. When slightly done invert the griddle and cook in dry heat till done.

① Khamiri Roti—p. 105
② Naan—p. 106

RANGEELA PULAO

INGREDIENTS :

3 cups rice
1 cup spinach (blanched and pureed)
1 cup tomato puree
1 cup curd
3-4 bay leaf
1½ tsp salt
1½ tsp *garam masala*
1 tsp green coriander (finely chopped)
3-4 cashew nuts
3-4 almonds
1½ tbsp oil

METHOD :

1. Clean and wash rice, divide into three equal portions and soak.
2. Divide oil, salt and *garam masala* also into three equal portions.
3. Heat one portion of the oil, add a bay leaf and allow to crackle. Add soaked rice and stir-fry. Add spinach puree, a portion of spices and a cup of water and pressure cook till done. This way you get green rice.
4. Similarly cook red rice with tomato puree.
5. Add whisked curd to the third part and cook white rice.
6. Arrange the rice on a serving platter in a pattern.
7. Garnish green part with almonds, red part with cashews and white part with coriander. Serve piping hot.

① Mewa Pulao—p. 110
② Rangeela Pulao—p. 109

MEWA PULAO

INGREDIENTS :

3 cups basmati rice
1 cup *makhanas* (puffed lotus seeds)
1 cup mixed dry fruits (raisins, *chiraunji*, melon seeds, etc.)
8-10 almonds
8-10 cashew nuts
½ cup dry coconut (grated)
5 cup milk
1 cup oil
3-4 green cardamoms
3-4 bay leaf
1 large onion (finely chopped) (optional)
3-4 threads saffron
1½ tsp salt
1 tsp *garam masala* (freshly ground)

METHOD :

1. Heat oil and stir-fry all the dry fruits except raisins and coconut.
2. Soak the saffron threads in milk and keep aside.
3. Heat the rest of the oil and add onions, cardamoms and bay leaf to it.
4. Add rice and stir-fry. Add a cup of water to the saffron milk and add to the cooking rice.
5. Stir in raisins, salt and *garam masala* and cook till just done.
6. Add *makhanas*, turn off the heat, cover (seal airtight if possible) and leave for 5-10 mts.
7. Serve hot garnished with finely chopped dry fruits.

BHARWAAN PARANTHA

INGREDIENTS :

1 cup whole wheat flour
¼ tsp salt
1 tsp pure *ghee*
oil for frying

For filling :

2 potatoes (boiled and mashed) or, 2 radish (grated and strained) or, 1 small cauliflower (grated) or, 100 grams cottage cheese *(paneer)* (mashed/ grated)
¼ tsp salt
¼ tsp red chilli powder
¼ tsp dried mango *(amchoor)* powder or *garam masala* powder or black pepper powder or *chaat masala* powder

METHOD :

1. Combine the filling with all the spices and mash between your palms.
2. Combine the flour with salt and *ghee.*
3. Knead a soft dough using water.
4. Divide the dough into balls of 3" (approx.) diameter and make a depression in the centre.
5. Stuff spoonfuls of filling and seal. Round again.
6. Roll out a little thick round *paranthas* and fry till reddish-brown on both sides on a hot griddle.
7. Serve crisp *paranthas* piping hot with pickle, butter and *raita.*

If you are stuffing the *paranthas* with grated radish then do not add salt in step-1. Instead sprinkle a pinch while stuffing each *parantha.*

MISSI ROTI

INGREDIENTS :

1 cup whole wheat flour
½ cup gram flour
¼ tsp salt
ghee for brushing

METHOD :

1. Combine the two flours and salt and sift together.
2. Knead to a semi-hard dough using water. Add water slowly otherwise the flour will get too wet.
3. Divide dough into balls of 2" (approx.) diameter roll out to *rotis* using a rolling pin.
4. Make *rotis* on a hot-dry griddle till crisp and swollen.
5. Brush the hot-aromatic *roti* with *ghee* and serve hot.

   You can enjoy this *roti* with jaggery.

MIXED PULAO

INGREDIENTS :

3 cups rice
1 cup cauliflower (small florets)
½ cup shelled peas (fresh)
1 cup potatoes (diced)
1 cup cottage cheese *(paneer)* (diced)
½ cup mushroom (chopped)
1 fresh spring onion (onion and stem separated)
5½ cup vegetable stock
1½ tsp salt
1 tsp *garam masala* powder
2½ tbsp oil
3-4 green chillies (finely chopped)
3-4 cloves
3-4 black cardamoms

METHOD :

1. Clean, wash and soak rice.
2. Heat 2 tbsp oil, fry all the vegetables separately (including green part of the spring onion) and keep aside.
3. Heat rest of the oil in a pressure cooker or a large deep pan and add cloves and cardamoms. Allow to crackle.
4. Chop (finely) onions, add to the crackling cardamom-cloves and stir-fry till red.
5. Add soaked rice and stir-fry till done.
6. Stir in stock, salt and *garam masala* powder, cover and cook till just done.
7. Remove the lid, stir in fried vegetables, cover again and simmer on low flame for 5-10 mts (or till done).
8. Turn off the heat and remove the lid only after 5-10 mts or just before serving.
9. Serve hot garnished with green chillies.

CREAM PULAO

INGREDIENTS :

3 cups rice
3 cups cream
¼ cup mint (dried and powdered)
1 cup puffed lotus seeds *(makhanas)* (fried and crushed)
1½ tsp salt
1½ tsp *garam masala* powder
1 large onion (finely chopped)
1 cup peanuts (shelled and fried)
1 cup processed cheese (grated)
1 tbsp onion (halved, finely sliced and stir-fried)
4 cups milk
4-5 green cardamoms
1½ tbsp butter or pure *ghee*

METHOD :

1. Clean, wash and soak rice.
2. Heat butter or *ghee*, add onion and stir-fry to reddish pink.
3. Add a cup of cream and stir-fry till the mixture leaves fat.
4. Add cardamoms and allow to crackle. Add rice and stir-fry.
5. Combine the milk with 1 cup cream and 1 cup water and add to the cooking rice.
6. Stir in salt, *garam masala* powder and mint powder, cover and cook till just done.
7. Remove the lid, stir in cheese and rest of the milk, cover again and simmer on low flame for 5-10 mts (or till done).
8. Turn off the heat and remove the lid only after 5-10 mts or just before serving.
9. Serve delicious and rich pulao on a rice plate garnished with crushed *makhanas,* peanuts and fried onions.

FRUIT PULAO

INGREDIENTS :

3 cups rice
5 cups mix-fruit juice
1 cup cream
1 cup pineapple (pieces)
1 cup green and black grapes (halved)
3-4 cloves
3-4 green cardamoms
a few bay-leaves
1 tbsp green coriander (finely chopped)
1 tsp *garam masala* powder
1½ tsp salt (or to taste)
2 tbsp oil

METHOD :

1. Clean, wash and soak rice.
2. Heat oil, add cloves, cardamoms and bay leaves, and allow to crackle.
3. Add soaked rice and stir-fry. Stir in fruit juice, 1 cup water and all the spices.
4. Cook the rice covered till just done.
5. Remove the lid, stir in the chopped fruits, cover again and simmer on low flame for 5-10 mts (or till done).
6. Turn off the heat and remove the lid only after 5-10 mts or just before serving.
7. Add the leftover fruits and arrange on a rice platter.
8. Add coriander to the cream and give it a gentle whisk.
9. Serve the fruity-tangy pulao garnished with coriander cream.

BEANS PULAO

INGREDIENTS :

¼ cup kidney beans (whole)
¼ cup whole Bengal gram
¼ cup black eye beans (whole)
¼ cup large white gram (whole)
2 cups tomato juice
2 onions (finely chopped)
3-4 green chillies
½" piece of ginger
3-4 cloves of garlic
1 tsp *garam masala* powder
1-1½ tsp salt
1 tsp coriander powder
¼ tsp turmeric powder
¾ tsp red chilli powder
oil (as required)
3-4 dried red chillies
5-6 green cardamoms
3 cups rice

METHOD :

1. Clean, wash the grams and beans and soak them overnight in 4 cups of water and salt.
2. Next morning pressure cook them without straining.
3. Chop and grind onions, ginger and garlic.
4. Heat oil, add dried red chillies and green cardamoms and allow to crackle.
5. Add the onion-garlic paste and stir-fry till pink. Add dry spices and cook till done.
6. Add steamed grams and beans (along with the stock), tomato juice and 1 cup of water and bring to a boil.
7. Add rice and cook till done.
8. Serve steaming garnished with green chillies.

DAHI PULAO

INGREDIENTS :

3 cups rice
1 cup *boondi*
5 cups curd (fresh creamy and thick)
1½ tsp salt
½ tsp mustard seeds
8-10 curry leaves
2 dried red chillies
½ tsp cummin seeds (roasted)
½ cup roasted sesame seeds
½ cup roasted peanuts
¼ cup cashew nuts (stir fried)
½ tbsp oil

METHOD :

1. Clean, wash and boil rice in water and half the salt.
2. Churn the curd and keep aside 3 cups. To the rest, add *boondi* and mix well.
3. Combine the remaining curd and boiled rice.
4. Heat oil, add dried red chillies, curry leaves and mustard seeds and allow to crackle. Then turn off the heat.
5. Add curd-rice mixture to it and add salt.
6. Stir in the curd-*boondi* mixture, mix well and sprinkle roasted cummin seeds.
7. Mix and serve on a rice platter garnished with roasted sesame seeds, peanuts and fried cashew.

FRIED RICE

INGREDIENTS :

- ¼ cup french beans (finely chopped)
- ¼ cup carrot (julienne)
- ¼ cup cabbage (shredded)
- 1 tbsp capsicum (finely chopped)
- 3 cups rice
- 1½ tbsp oil
- 1½ tsp salt
- ½ tsp black pepper (freshly ground)
- 1½ tsp soya sauce
- 1 tsp vinegar

METHOD :

1. Clean, wash and soak rice.
2. Heat a tbsp of oil and stir-fry the chopped vegetables separately and keep aside.
3. Add ½ tbsp oil and salt and cook the rice till just done.
4. Turn off the heat, remove the lid and toss rice so that every grain is moisture free and separate.
5. Heat a wok or *karahi*, combine fried vegetables and rice and toss on high heat for stir mixing and re-heating.
6. Sprinkle pepper, vinegar and soya sauce evenly on top and give another toss on high heat.
7. Mix well and serve hot.

MUSHROOM TAMATAR PULAO (BIRYANI)

INGREDIENTS :

350 grams fresh mushroom (sliced)
500 grams tomatoes (pureed)
4 large tomatoes (sliced)
3 cups rice (soaked)
3 large onions (halved and sliced)
3-4 cloves of garlic
½" piece of ginger
1½ tsp salt
1 tsp coriander powder
½ tsp turmeric powder
½ tsp red chilli powder
¾ tsp *garam masala* powder
½ cup oil
1½ cup fresh green coriander (chopped)

METHOD :

1. Grind together ⅓ of the sliced onions, ginger and garlic.
2. Heat half the oil, stir-fry sliced onions till golden and add mushrooms. Season with salt and stir-fry till done. Keep aside.
3. Heat rest of the oil and stir-fry onion mixture till pink. Add salt and other dry spices and stir-fry. Add rice, mix and stir-fry again.
4. Measure tomato juice and add water to complete 6 cups. Add this to the rice, stir and allow to cook.
5. Cover and simmer on low flame for 5-10 mts (or till done). Turn off the heat but do not remove the lid for another 5-10 mts.
6. In a large-deep heavy bottomed pan arrange a layer of tomato rice (1/3 of total) followed by a layer of cooked mushrooms. Again layer the pan with tomato rice and layer tomatoes on top. Finish with a final layer of rice and leftover mushroom and tomatoes on top.
7. Sprinkle coriander and cover (seal with dough if possible).
8. Cook the *biryani* on very low heat (low flame or coal fire or oven) for 5-15 mts.
9. Serve the aromatic *biryani* steaming hot.

PANEER-PAALAK SPECIAL PULAO

INGREDIENTS :

5 cups spinach (blanched and pureed)
1 cup tomato juice (strained)
2½ cups cottage cheese *(paneer)* (grated)
3 cups rice
2½ onions (halved and thinly sliced)
4-5 cloves of garlic (ground)
½" piece of ginger (ground)
3-4 bay leaf
2-3 black cardamoms
2½ tbsp oil
1 tsp salt
1½ tsp coriander powder
½ tsp turmeric powder
1 tsp red chilli powder
1 tsp *garam masala* powder

METHOD :

1. Clean, wash and soak rice.
2. Heat oil, add black cardamoms and bay leaf and allow to crackle. Add onions and stir-fry till pink.
3. Strain out some of the fried onion on brown paper as it soaks the excess oil.
4. Add ginger-garlic paste and stir-fry to golden brown.
5. Season with salt, add all the dry spices, sprinkle a little water and stir-fry till done. Add rice and stir-fry.
6. Add tomato juice and boil. Add pureed spinach and allow to cook till just done.
7. Stir in 2 cups of grated cheese and continue stirring.
8. Cover and simmer on low flame for 5-10 mts (or till done).
9. Turn off the heat but do not remove the lid for 5-10 mts or until serving.
10. Serve hot garnished with leftover cheese and fried onions.

NAASHTE

(Snacks)

PAALAK (SPINACH) PANCAKE

INGREDIENTS :

1 cup all purpose flour *(maida)*
¼ tsp baking powder
2 cups milk
½ tsp salt
½ tsp black pepper powder
1 cup spinach *(paalak)* (finely chopped)
½ cup processed cheese (grated)
oil for frying

METHOD :

1. Combine and sieve flour, baking powder, salt and black pepper.
2. Gradually, add milk and make a smooth batter taking care that lumps do not form.
3. Add a tsp of oil to it and use a little water if the batter is too thick.
4. Heat the pan and spread a tsp of oil on it.
5. Sprinkle water and wipe with a cloth.
6. Spread 2 tbsp batter to make the pancake.
7. Sprinkle chopped spinach.
8. Pour oil on the edges and turn over the pancake.

Once done sprinkle cheese and serve hot with sauce.

CUTLET

INGREDIENTS :

2 potatoes (boiled)
1 cup cottage cheese *(paneer)* (grated)
1 cup peas (shelled, cooked and ground)
2-3 green chillies (finely chopped)
1 tbsp green coriander (finely chopped)
1½ cup bread crumbs
¾ tsp salt
½ tsp red chilli powder
oil for frying

METHOD :

1. Mash or grate potatoes and combine with pea paste.
2. Add green chillies, coriander and grated *paneer*, season with salt and pepper, mash and mix well.
3. Spread bread crumbs on kitchen paper.
4. Make cutlets from the potato mixture in desired shapes and roll them in bread crumbs.
5. Deep fry in hot oil and remove on kitchen paper.
6. Serve hot with sauce or green coriander *chutney*.

NOODLES CHOWMEIN

INGREDIENTS :

2 cups noodles (boiled or steamed)
½ cup cabbage (shredded)
¼ cup carrot (julienned)
¼ cup onions (halved and finely sliced)
¼ cup beans (fresh and finely chopped)
½ capsicum (chopped lengthwise)
¾ tsp salt
¼ tsp mono-sodium glutamate
½ tsp black pepper (freshly ground)
2 tbsp vinegar
2 tbsp soya sauce
chilli sauce to accompany
1 omelette (ready, one egg only) (optional)
2½ tbsp oil

METHOD :

1. Heat oil in a wok or *karahi* and stir-fry onions over high flame.
2. Add rest of the vegetables and stir-fry on high flame till crisp.
3. Strain out the crisp-fried vegetables and add steamed noodles to the leftover hot oil.
4. Toss the noodles on high heat.
5. Add vegetables, vinegar, soya sauce and mono-sodium glutamate, mix well, season with salt and pepper and toss over high flame.
6. Cut the omelette into strips.
7. Serve piping hot garnished with omelette strips on top.

MATAR BURGER

INGREDIENTS :

250 grams peas (fresh and shelled)
¼ tsp salt
¼ tsp red chilli powder
¼ tsp dried mango *(amchoor)* powder
1 small potato (boiled and grated)
¼ cup bread crumbs
oil for frying
4 large burger buns
4-6 onion slices
4-6 tomato slices
1 cup cabbage (shredded)
½ cup soft cheese (processed) or mayonnaise

METHOD :

1. Heat a tsp of oil, add the shelled peas and spices, cook till done and grind to a fine paste.
2. Add potatoes, mix well and make cutlets of desired shapes.
3. Roll them in bread crumbs, fry and remove on kitchen paper or brown paper.
4. Combine cheese/mayonnaise with shredded cabbage to form a spread.
5. Slit the buns horizontally to divide into two halves and fry them lightly on a hot-greased griddle.
6. Assemble the burger, by sandwiching between the two bun-halves, a layer of spread followed by onion and tomato slices and finally a pea cutlet.
7. Wrap the burgers in paper napkins.
8. Serve the perfect bite with tomato and chilli sauces.

① Matar Burger—p. 124
② Noodles Chowmein—p. 123

RANG-RANGEELA DHOKLA

INGREDIENTS :

1½ cup gram flour *(besan)* or semolina *(suji)*
2½ cup sour curd
½ tsp salt
½ tsp red chilli powder
½ tsp soda-bi-carb
2 green chillies (finely chopped)
1 tomato (finely sliced)
4-5 beans (fresh and chopped)
4-5 cauliflower florets
½ capsicum (chopped)
½ carrot (diced)
3-4 spinach leaves (shredded)
1 small onion (finely chopped)
1 tbsp shelled peas

METHOD :

1. Combine sour curd, salt and red chilli powder and mix well.
2. Clean, wash and strain chopped vegetables.
3. Combine the spiced curd and semolina/flour, mix well and add the strained vegetables.
4. Sprinkle soda and mix well.
5. Transfer to greased baking or steaming dish.
6. Fill a large heavy-bottomed pan with water and set to boil.
7. Support filled baking dish over boiling water, cover and cook for 25-30 mts.
8. Check by poking the *dhokla* with a knitting needle or a knife. If it comes out clean with nothing sticking to it, the *dhokla* is ready.
9. You may de-mould and serve it on a platter garnished to your liking.

① Halwa-Mathari—p. 128
② Rang-Rangeela Dhokla—p. 127

HALWA-MATHARI

INGREDIENTS :

For halwa :

2 cups semolina *(suji)*

1½ cups sugar

1 cup pure *ghee*

5-6 cups water (approx. triple the quantity of semolina)

3-4 green cardamoms (powdered)

8-10 raisins

5-7 almonds (flaked or finely chopped)

grated dry coconut (optional)

For mathari :

1 cup all purpose flour *(maida)*

1 cup semolina

4 tbsp pure *ghee*

¾ tsp salt

¼ tsp thyme seeds

oil for frying

METHOD :

1. To make *halwa* heat *ghee* in a *karahi,* add semolina and stir-fry till golden pink.
2. Add water and raisins and stir till semolina imbibes water.
3. Add sugar when thick and keep on stirring till done.
4. Sprinkle cardamom powder, almonds and grated coconut on top.
5. To make *mathari* combine semolina, flour and salt and sieve together. Add thyme seeds and mix well.
6. Add *ghee* and knead using water to make a bit stiff dough.
7. Divide into small-equal balls and roll out to small a bit thick *matharis.*
8. Poke some of them with a knife tip or a fork, deep fry till golden pink and remove on absorbent paper.
9. Enjoy steaming hot *matharis* with mouth-watering *halwa.*

PANEERI SAMOSA

INGREDIENTS :

2 cups all purpose flour *(maida)*
4 tbsp pure *ghee*
½ tsp salt
2 cups fresh cottage cheese *(paneer)*
¼ cups raisins and cashew nuts
1 large onion (finely chopped)
½ tsp black pepper (freshly ground)
oil for frying
finely chopped green chillies and green coriander (to taste)

METHOD :

1. Combine flour and salt and sieve. Add *ghee* and knead to a soft dough. Keep covered with a moist cloth.
2. Heat oil and stir-fry onions to golden. Add *paneer*, spices and raisins and stir-fry till done.
3. Coarsely crush cashew nuts, add to the cooking *paneer* and stir till done and dry enough for filling.
4. Divide the dough into 6-8 equal balls and roll out using a rolling pin to make very thin circular sheets.
5. Divide each sheet into two semi-circular halves using a sharp knife.
6. Join one end of the straight side to the other to form a cone and seal the joint by moistening the overlapping edges.
7. Stuff each cone with spoonfuls of *paneer* filling and seal by moistening.
8. Deep-fry triangular *samosas* in hot oil on low flame till golden pink.
9. Serve hot with tamarind sauce, coriander *chutney* and *chhole*.

SABZION KI PIE (VEGETABLE PIE)

INGREDIENTS :

2½ cups all purpose flour (*maida*)
4 tbsp pure *ghee*
¾ tsp salt
½ tsp black pepper (freshly ground)
½ cup processed cheese (grated)
6 tbsp ice-chilled water

For the filling :

any dry vegetarian mixture—potatoes or peas or scrambled eggs/ coarsely ground soya nuggets or sauteed mushrooms or vegetarian noodles
4 large potatoes (mashed)
1 cup shelled peas (boiled)
10-15 mushrooms (quartered)
4 large onions (halved and sliced)
½ cup processed cheese (grated)
¾ tsp salt
½ tsp black pepper (freshly ground)
1 tbsp oil

METHOD :

1. Heat oil, add chopped onions and stir-fry till pink. Add mushrooms, stir till done and add mashed potatoes and peas.
2. Season with salt and pepper, add cheese and stir-fry till done.
3. To prepare pie crust combine all the dry ingredients, add cheese and knead with ice-chilled water.
4. Divide into two parts and roll them to make 2 pastry sheets approx. ¼ cm thick.
5. Grease an aluminium or glassware baking (pie) dish and line it with one sheet taking care to cover the walls of the dish.
6. Spoon entire stuffing in to the lined dish, cover with the second sheet and seal by joining the ends of both sheets.
7. Poke with a fork or a knife in patterns and twist the joints in shapes.
8. Bake the pie in a preheated oven for about an hour.
9. Serve the steaming pie with sauces and *chutney*.

CHEELE

INGREDIENTS :

1 cup semolina or gram flour or green gram *(moong dhuli)* (washed, skinned, soaked and ground to paste)
½ tsp salt
½ tsp red chilli powder
1 tbsp green coriander (finely chopped)
onion-tomato salad with lemon juice and salt
oil for frying

METHOD :

1. If using semolina or flour, use water to make a thick batter first, otherwise directly add coriander, salt and chilli powder and mix well.
2. Heat and grease a skillet or griddle, sprinkle a few drops of water and wipe off with a clean cloth.
3. Spread two spoonfuls of batter on the griddle and sprinkle a few drops of oil along the edges. Fry the *cheela* on both sides to golden brown in a simillar way.
4. Serve crisp *Cheela* with salad stuffed in it or with it.

HARIYALI KHASTA KACHAURI

INGREDIENTS :

3 cups all purpose flour *(maida)*
3 tbsp pure *ghee*
¾ tsp salt
¼ tsp baking powder

For filling :
250 grams green Bengal gram
½ tsp salt
½ tsp red chilli powder
¼tsp fennel seeds
¼ tsp coriander seeds
2-3 green chillies (finely chopped)
¼ tsp ginger (finely chopped)
oil for frying
luke warm water for kneading the dough

METHOD :

1. Heat a tbsp of oil, add coriander and fennel seeds, allow to crackle. Add the gram, salt and red chilli powder and cook till done.
2. Sprinkle chopped chillies and ginger, mix well and leave the filling to cool down.
3. Combine flour, salt and baking powder and sieve together.
4. Add *ghee* and knead using luke warm water to a soft dough.
5. Divide it into small balls of equal size, flatten each ball, keep a spoonful of filling in the centre and seal.
6. Roll each stuffed dough-ball a bit with a rolling pin and deep fry on low flame till golden and crisp to make *kachauris*.
7. Serve with *chutney* and *aaloo ki sabzi*.

PAUSHTIC IDLI

INGREDIENTS :

2 cups *motth*/ green gram *(moong)* (sprouted)
1 cup black gram *(urad dhuli)* (washed and skinned)
1 cup rice
1 tsp salt
½ tsp soda-bi-carb

METHOD :

1. Clean, wash and soak rice and black gram overnight.
2. Strain, wash and grind together to make *idli* batter, add salt and keep aside.
3. When the batter has fermented and risen to at least double it's volume (approx. 5-7 hours in summers and 12-14 hours in winters) add sprouted gram and mix with a light hand.
4. Grease an *idli* stand and spoon the batter in all the slots/ moulds. Steam-cook the *idlis*.
5. Enjoy steaming hot *idlis* with *sambhar* and *nariyal ki chutney*.

Nariyal (Coconut) Chutney :

Coarsely chop the white part of half a coconut and grind in a grinder together with a cup of curd, half a cup of roasted and skinned whole Bengal gram, 3-4 cloves of garlic and ½ a tsp of salt.

Prepare tempering as : heat a tbsp of oil, add 1-2 dried red chillies and ¼ tsp salt and allow to crackle. Temper the *chutney* and serve with *dosa*, *idli*, etc or otherwise.

PAV-BHAJI

INGREDIENTS :

6 large *pav* (buns)
100 grams butter

For the *bhaji* :

2 cups large white gram *(chhole)* (boiled and mashed)
4 potatoes (boiled and mashed)
1 cup cabbage (grated)
½ cup tomato puree
2 onions (halved and sliced)
¼ cup cauliflower (grated)
¼ cup peas (shelled and crushed)
1 tsp turmeric powder
2 tbsp *pav-bhaji masala*
1 tsp red chilli powder
1 tsp salt
100 grams cottage cheese *(paneer)* (diced)
10-12 cashew nuts
onion-tomato salad, green chillies (finely chopped) and lemons to accompany

METHOD :

1. Heat 1½ tbsp of butter in a *karahi* and stir-fry the onions till done. Add turmeric powder, *pav-bhaji masala*, red chilli powder, salt and ¼ cup water and stir-fry till done.
2. Stir in tomato puree, mashed gram, potato, cauliflower, peas and cabbage and stir to mash and mix.
3. Stir in a tbsp of butter and the *bhaji* is ready.
4. Slit the *pav* (buns) horizontally and grill inside-out on a hot griddle greased with butter.
5. Garnish *bhaji* with cashews and diced cheese and sprinkle lemon juice on top.
6. Serve delicious-aromatic *bhaji* with *pav* and salad.

ALL-IN-ONE SANDWICH

INGREDIENTS :

1 slice processed cheese
2 slices large tomatoes (finely sliced)
2 slices cucumbers (finely sliced-lengthwise)
¼ cup cheese spread
¼ cup cabbage (shredded or grated)
1 round potato cutlet
1 omelette (single egg)
salt and pepper to taste
butter (to requirement)
sandwich bread (sliced and crust removed) (to requirement)

METHOD :

1. Butter all the slices and season them with salt and pepper.
2. Combine cheese spread and cabbage to make cabbage spread.
3. Sandwich all the ingredients layer by layer, with a buttered and seasoned bread slice separating each, in a order to your liking.
4. Wrap the massive layered sandwich in a moistened towel.
5. Serve the set all-in-one sandwich with coffee and cookies.

UPMA

INGREDIENTS :

1 cup semolina *(suji)*
1 tbsp *ghee* or oil
3-4 curry leaves
¼ tsp mustard seeds
½ cup peas (shelled)
½ cup cauliflower florets
1 potato (boiled and diced)
1 tomato (finely chopped)
¼ cup peanuts (shelled and roasted/fried)
½ tsp black gram *(urad dhuli)* (washed and skinned)
½ tsp Bengal gram *(chana dal)* (washed and skinned)
¾ tsp salt
½ tsp red chilli powder

METHOD :

1. Dry roast the semolina to pink in a hot *karahi*.
2. Heat oil or *ghee* in a *karahi*, stir-fry the grams, add mustard and curry leaves and allow to crackle.
3. Add salt, red chilli powder and water (apporx. triple the amount of semolina) and bring to a boil.
4. Gradually add roasted semolina and continue stirring till it imbibes water and swells out.
5. Add peanuts, mix well and add finely chopped green chillies and coriander if desired.
6. Serve piping hot with sauces of your choice.

PAUSHTIC DALIYA

INGREDIENTS :

2 cups broken wheat *(daliya)*
1 cup peas (shelled)
2 eggs (boiled and chopped) (optional)
¼ cup green gram *(moong dhuli)* (washed and skinned)
¼ cup beans (fresh-chopped)
¼ carrot (finely sliced or diced)
¼ cup cauliflower florets
1 tomato (finely chopped)
¾ tsp salt
½ tsp black pepper (freshly ground)
1½ tbsp *ghee* or oil
2 cloves or a pinch of cummin seeds

METHOD :

1. Clean, wash and soak the gram.
2. Clean, wash and keep aside the wheat.
3. Heat *ghee* or oil, add cloves or cummin seeds and allow to crackle.
4. Add wheat and soaked gram and stir-fry till pink.
5. Add all the chopped vegetables and stir-fry. Add 4-5 cups (approx.) of water, season with salt and pepper and pressure cook till *daliya* is done.
6. Add or garnish with chopped eggs and sprinkle a tbsp of *ghee* on top just before serving.
7. Serve the nutritious *daliya* with sauces and *chutneys* of your selection.

DESSERT

NUT AND FRUIT KHEER

INGREDIENTS :

1 litre full cream milk
½ cup rice
3-4 green cardamom (ground)
½ cup mixed dry fruits (cashew nuts, almond, raisins, *makhanas* and melon seeds)
2 bananas (ripe)
10-12 grapes
½ cup tinned pineapple (chopped)
¾ cup sugar

METHOD :

1. Clean, wash and soak rice.
2. Bring the milk to a boil, add soaked rice and allow to simmer stirring in-between.
3. Add ground cardamoms and keep on stirring. Scrap the *malai* (milk fat) settling on the vessel walls and add to the simmering *kheer*.
4. Add raisins and *makhanas* and allow them to swell out. Continue simmering till thick and keep on scraping the sides.
5. Add the rest of dry fruits and sugar and mix well.
6. Remove from heat, chill a bit and serve cold along with chopped fruits.

AAM KI KULFI

INGREDIENTS :

2 litre milk
2 cups mango pulp
1 cup mango (diced)
¼ cup almonds (finely chopped/flakes)
a pinch of saffron threads
½ cup thick cream (whisked)
1 cup sugar

METHOD :

1. Boil the milk and keep boiling till it reduces to half (leave a *kalchhi* or ladle in the boiling milk so that it does not spill).
2. Keep stirring and scraping the sides in-between.
3. Stir in sugar and saffron dissolved in half cup of water, remove from heat and allow to cool.
4. Fold-in the puffed cream and chopped mango and almonds.
5. Transfer to *kulfi* moulds and set to freeze.
6. De-mould and serve with cool *faluda*.

MISHTI DAHI

INGREDIENTS :

½ litre milk
2 tbsp sugar
8-10 grapes
½ cup bananas (finely chopped)
½ tsp green cardamom (ground)
2 tbsp curd

METHOD :

1. Heat milk, add cardamom powder and dissolve in the sugar.
2. Remove from heat.
3. Spread chopped fruits and curd in an earthenware curd vessel.
4. Pour the luke warm milk and allow the curd to set.
5. When set, chill the *Mishti Dahi* and enjoy it on a sultry summer afternoon.

SHAHI FIRNI

INGREDIENTS :

½ cup rice (dried and ground)
1½ litre milk
¾ cup sugar
½ tsp green cardamom (ground)
2 tbsp almond (flakes/ coarsely ground)
Pistachios (finely chopped) for garnishing
faluda dipped in *kewra* water to accompany

METHOD :

1. Add cardamom powder to the milk and allow to boil.
2. Add ground rice to the boiling milk and keep stirring till it thickens.
3. Add almonds and sugar to it and refrigerate.
4. Fold in *faluda* and *kewra* water.
5. Serve chilled.

This traditional delicacy can be best enjoyed in earthenware cups/bowls.

JUICY PINEAPPLE CUP

INGREDIENTS :

3 tbsp cornflour
300 ml water
1 cup sugar
400 grams pineapple (finely chopped)
1½ cup cream (whisked)
5-6 cherries for decoration

METHOD :

1. Dissolve cornflour in a little water taking care that lumps do not form.
2. Heat the rest of the water, add sugar and chopped pineapple and cook till it is tender.
3. Remove from heat and allow to cool.
4. Blend in a blender, strain out the juice to the last drop by applying pressure and reheat it.
5. Stir in the cornflour solution, simmer for 3-5 mts, remove from fire and allow to cool.
6. Fold-in the whisked cream with a delicate hand and refrigerate to set.
7. Decorate with cherries (or red coloured jam) and serve the chilled-refreshing juicy pineapple cup.

① Shahi Firni—p. 141
② Juicy Pineapple Cup—p. 142

JELLY

INGREDIENTS :

1 packet strawberry jelly
2 tbsp sugar (powder)
1 cup thick cream (whisked)
1½ cup mixed fruits (finely chopped)
1 tsp lemon juice

METHOD :

1. Prepare and set the jelly as according to directions on the package.
2. Sprinkle lemon juice on chopped fruits.
3. Add sugar to the whisked cream and puff.
4. Spread some of the mixed fruits in individual serving bowls followed by lots of jelly.
5. Spoon sweet puffed cream on top, garnish with leftover fruit and serve chilled.

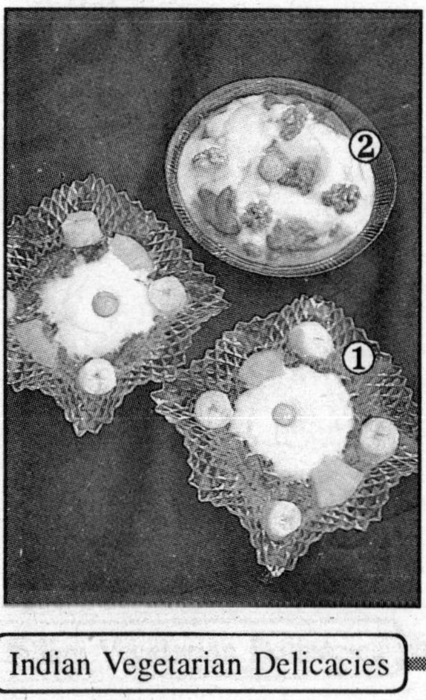

① Jelly—p. 145
② Choc-Chocolate—p. 146

CHOC-CHOCOLATE

INGREDIENTS :

5 cups milk
2½ tbsp chocolate powder
3 tbsp cocoa powder
½ tbsp coffee powder
¾ cup sugar
1½ tbsp cornflour
1 tsp chocolate essence
80 grams chocolate bar (broken to pieces)
2 cups sweet cream (puffed and chilled)
½ cup walnuts (coarsely ground)

METHOD :

1. Keep aside ¾ cup of milk and boil the rest.
2. Combine sugar, cocoa powder, coffee powder, cornflour and chocolate powder and make a thick paste with ¾ cup of milk.
3. Slowly stir this paste into the boiling milk so as to avoid lump formation and keep stirring till the milk thickens.
4. Remove from heat and cool.
5. Pour half the cold chocolate in a serving dish, stir in chocolate essence and arrange a layer of chocolate pieces and half the walnuts.
6. Pour the rest of the ready chocolate and top it with a layer of puffed cream.
7. Garnish with rest of the chocolate pieces and walnuts and refrigerate.
8. Serve chilled.

CUSTARD SUPREME

INGREDIENTS :

500 ml milk
2½ tbsp vanilla custard powder
2 tbsp sugar
1 cup fresh cream
4 bananas
1 tsp lemon juice
4 pineapple rings
1 cup mixed grapes and pomegranate seeds
2 oranges
¼ cup mixed dry fruits (almonds, raisins and cashews)

METHOD :

1. Add 1½ tbsp sugar to the milk and let it boil.
2. Add remaining sugar and custard powder to half a glass of water and make a thick lump-free solution.
3. Turn down the flame, slowly stir in the solution and keep on stirring till it thickens.
4. Remove from fire, cool and refrigerate.
5. Chop all the fruits, combine with grapes and pomegranate and sprinkle lemon juice on top.
6. Fold the cold whisked cream into chilled custard and add dry fruits.
7. Serve the rich creamy custard with sweet and sour fruits.

VANILLA ICE CREAM

INGREDIENTS :

2½ cups cream
1 tbsp custard power
½ cup + 2 tbsp sugar
1 tsp gelatine
1 egg [yolk (yellow) and albumin (white) parts separated]
½ cup almonds and peanuts
1 tsp vanilla essence

METHOD :

1. Whisk the egg yolk till fluffy and light, combine sugar and custard powder and make a thick paste with the whisked eggs.
2. Smooth it with a little cream.
3. Luke warm the remaining cream, pour (in a slender streak) into the beaten egg yolk and whisk.
4. Heat cream and simmer till thick. Remove from heat and cool.
5. Whisk the egg white till frothy and fluffy.
6. Dissolve gelatine in ½ cup luke warm water and allow to swell.
7. Combine soaked gelatine and whisked eggs and whisk.
8. Add to the cream mixture and mix well. Cover and freeze.
9. Remove the cover and churn when half frozen, freeze again.
10. Melt 2 tbsp of sugar and heat till golden brown. Stir in the dry fruits and let the caramel coat them and quickly remove from heat. Cool the caramelised nuts and coarsely chop them.
11. Take out the half-frozen ice cream, add caramalised nuts and vanilla essence churn and freeze again covered with tin foil.

If you don't want to use egg then you can also make the ice cream without it.

CAKE JELLYTARD PUDDING

INGREDIENTS :

1 eggless cake
1 cup grapes (halved)
1 cup canned pineapple (chopped)
2 cups vanilla custard (ready)
2 cups strawberry jelly (ready)
1 cup ice cream

METHOD :

1. Scoop out a cavity in the centre of the cake using a large spoon or cup.
2. Combine ¼ of the fruits and ½ cup jelly and pour into the centre of the cake. Fill the cavity and set the cake to freeze.
3. Refrigerate rest of the jelly and allow it to set.
4. Remove the cake from freezer and fill the remaining gap with quarter cup custard.
5. Place the cake in the centre of a serving dish, surround with jelly and refrigerate to set.
6. Arrange the remaining custard on top and top it with fruits.
7. Decorate with grapes and spoon ice cream on top. Serve chilled.

ORANGE SPONGE PUDDING

INGREDIENTS :

1 cup butter
1 cup sugar
1½ cup all purpose flour *(maida)*
2½ tsp baking powder
2 eggs (whisked till white)
2 tsp orange essence
2 oranges (segments-peeled and seeded)
milk (according to requirement)

METHOD :

1. Combine sugar and butter and whisk till light and creamy white.
2. Gradually and slowly, add the whisked eggs while whisking the sugar-butter mixture.
3. Sift the flour and baking powder together and add to the mixture. Mix well.
4. Roll the skinned orange segments in flour and add to the mixture along with orange essence. Fold with a gentle hand and stir in enough milk to give it a flowing consistency.
5. Grease a pudding tin, fill it with the mixture, cover with an aluminium foil or butter paper and steam it for 1-1½ hour.
6. Invert the tin on the serving platter and serve topped with chilled custard or cold-sweet cream.

THANDI RICE PUDDING

INGREDIENTS :

½ litre milk
¼ cup rice
1½ tbsp sugar
3-4 green cardamoms (freshly powdered)
1 cup chilled cream
2 cups pomegranate and apple juice
1 cup seasonal fruit (any) (finely chopped)
1½ tsp gelatine

METHOD :

1. Heat the milk, add powdered cardamoms to it and let it boil. Leave a ladle or heavy spoon in the pan so that it boils but does not spill over.
2. Clean and wash rice and add to the boiling milk.
3. When rice is tender and milk has thickened stir in sugar, remove from heat and chill.
4. Dissolve the gelatine in ½ cup luke warm water and add to the fruit juice. Mix well and freeze till set.
5. Set the chilled *kheer* with chilled cream and crushed fruit ice in a pudding tin topped with chopped fruits.
6. Serve chilled and set as a dessert following a hearty meal.

BAKED SEB PUDDING

INGREDIENTS :

4 apples (fresh and juicy)
4 tbsp sugar (powdered)
50 grams fresh white butter
1 cup vanilla custard (ready)
1 cup strawberry ice cream
½ cup mixed dry fruits (finely chopped)
60 ml water

METHOD :

1. Wipe apples with a clean cloth.
2. Scoop out the seeds using a potato eye remover or something similar.
3. Heat a tbsp of butter and stir-fry the dry fruits.
4. Sprinkle the powdered sugar, give few dashes of water (splash some water) and stir the dry fruits quickly to coat them with sugar.
5. Fill apples with candied dry fruits, brush with butter and arrange in a shallow baking dish.
6. Fill the dish with water and set in a preheated oven to bake for about 40 mts. In-between spoon the cooking liquid on apples and rotate the apples for an even bake.
7. Add the left over cooking liquid to the custard.
8. Arrange apples in a serving dish, spoon the custard in-between.
9. Top the apples with ice cream and serve cool.

BHUTTE KA HALWA

INGREDIENTS :

2 cups corn kernels
500 ml milk
1 tbsp sugar
3-4 green cardamoms (freshly powdered)
almonds and raisins (to liking)
2 tbsp pure *ghee*

METHOD :

1. Boil corn kernels for 10 mts and grind coarsely.
2. Heat a tbsp of *ghee* and stir-fry the ground kernels a bit. Stir in the milk and allow to boil and reduce.
3. When milk is reduced to nill add the rest of the *ghee* and stir.
4. Add cardamom powder, raisins, and sugar and stir-fry till raisins swell out and a characteristic aroma rises.
5. Serve garnished with chopped or flaked almonds and silver foil.

FRUIT CREAM

INGREDIENTS :

½ kg cream
2 tbsp sugar
1 lemon
1 tsp vanilla essence
seasonal mixed fruits (bananas, apple orange segments, grapes, mangoes, *litchi*, plums, etc)
1 cup milk

METHOD :

1. Dissolve sugar in water and add to the cream.
2. Squeeze in lemon and add vanilla essence to the cream and chill.
3. Peel, seed and chop fruits and fold into the chilled cream.
4. Garnish with jam, coloured candies, etc and serve refreshingly chilled.

GLOSSARY

Dry Fruits

1.	Almonds	*Badam*
2.	Coconut	*Nariyal*
3.	Dry Coconut	*Kopra*
4.	Groundnut/peanut	*Moongphalli*
5.	Raisins	*Kishmish*
6.	Pistachio	*Pista*
7.	Cashew nut	*Kaju*
8.	Walnut	*Akhroat*
9.	Lotus-seed Puffs	*Makhana*
10.	Chilgoza	*Chilgoza*
11.	Chiraunji	

Cereals and Pulses

1.	Wheat	*Gehun*
2.	Millet	*Bajra*
3.	Vermicelli	*Sevian*
4.	Semolina	*Suji*
5.	Sago	*Sabudana*
6.	Rice	*Chawal*
7.	Red gram	*Arhar dal*
8.	Green gram	*Moong*
9.	Lentil	*Masoor*
10.	Black gram	*Urad*
11.	Bengal gram	*Chana*
12.	Barley	*Jowar*
13.	Corn	*Makkai*
14.	Refined flour	*Maida*
15.	Gram flour	*Besan*
16.	Millet flour	*Bajre ka atta*
17.	Whole meal flour	*Atta*
18.	Large white gram	*Kabuli chana*
19.	Red kidney bean	*Rajma*
20.	Black eye bean	*Rawa/Rungi*
21.	Rice (pressed)	*Chidwa*
22.	Rice puffs	*Murmure*
23.	Bengal gram (whole)	*Chhole*
24.	Green gram (whole)	*Moong*
25.	Motth beans	*Motth*
26.	Broken wheat	*Daliya*

Vegetables

1.	Onion	*Pyaz*
2.	Potato	*Aaloo*
3.	Tomato	*Tamatar*
4.	Turnip	*Shalgam*
5.	Spinach	*Paalak*
6.	Yam	*Zimikand*
7.	Sweet potato	*Shakarkand*
8.	White gourd	*Lauki*
9.	Spring onion	*Hara pyaz*
10.	Beetroot	*Chukandar*
11.	Beans	*Sem*
12.	Bitter gourd	*Karela*
13.	Capsicum	*Shimla mirch*
14.	Carrot	*Gajar*
15.	Snake gourd	*Chachinda*
16.	Radish	*Mooli*
17.	Mushroom	*Kukarmutta/ Guchi*
18.	Green peas	*Matar*
19.	Ladies finger/okra	*Bhindi*
20.	Pumpkin	*Kaddu*
21.	Round gourd	*Tinda*
22.	Jackfruit	*Kathal*
23.	Ridge gourd	*Turai*
24.	Brinjal/Eggplant/ Aubergine	*Baigan*
25.	Cabbage	*Bandgobhi/ Pattagobhi*
26.	Cauliflower	*Phoolgobhi*
27.	Celery	*Ajwain leaves*
28.	Fenugreek leaves	*Methi*
29.	French beans	*Phrans bean*

30. Mint	*Podina*
31. Coriander	*Dhaniya*
32. Cucumber	*Kheera/kakri*
33. Ginger	*Adrak*
34. Garlic	*Lahsun*
35. Green chilli	*Hari mirch*
36. Drumstick	*Saijan ki phalli*
37. Colocasia	*Arvi*
38. Bamboo shoots	*Baans*
39. Bathua leaves	*Bathua saag*
40. Lettuce leaves	*Salad ke patte*
41. Mustard leaves	*Sarson saag*
42. Dill	*Soy saag*
43. Lotus seeds	*Kamal ke beege*
44. Cluster beans	*Guer ki phalli*
45. Lotus stem	*Kamalgatta*
46. Parwar	*Parwal*
47. Plantain	*Kela (hara)*
48. Water chestnut	*Shinghara*

Herbs and Spices

1. Aniseed	*Sauf*
2. Saffron	*Kesar*
3. Nutmeg	*Jaiphal*
4. Mustard seeds	*Sarson/rai*
5. Mace	*Javitri*
6. Jaggery	*Gur*
7. Asafoetida	*Heeng*
8. Bay leaf	*Tej patta*
9. Black pepper/ pepper corns	*Kali mirch*
10. Red chilli	*Lal mirch*
11. Turmeric	*Haldi*
12. Coriander seeds	*Dhaniya*
13. Cummin	*Jeera*
14. Tymol seeds/thyme	*Ajwain*
15. Sesame seed	*Til*
16. Dried mango powder	*Amchoor*
17. Poppy seeds	*Khuskhus*
17. Fenugreek seeds	*Methidana*
18. Dry ginger	*Sonth*
19. Cloves	*Laung*
20. Cinnamon	*Dalchini*
21. Baking soda	*Khane ka soda*
22. Parsley	*Ajmod ka patta*
23. Curry leaves	*Meethi neem/ Curry patta*
24. Arrowroot	*Arrawroot*
25. Basil	*Tulsi*
26. Caraway seeds	*Shahjeera*
27. Cardamoms	*Elaichi*
28. Tamarind	*Imli*
29. Marjoram	*Bantulsi*
30. Onion seeds	*Kalonji*
31. Vinegar	*Sirka*

Fruits

1. Pineapple	*Annanaas*
2. Orange	*Santra*
3. Lemon	*Meetha nimbu*
4. Lime	*Nimbu*
5. Pears	*Nashpati*
6. Pomegranates	*Anar*
7. Apple	*Seb*
8. Grapes	*Angoor*
9. Apricots	*Khubani*
10. Fig	*Anjeer*
11. Banana	*Kela*
12. Olives	*Jaitun*
13. Peaches	*Arhu*
14. Guava	*Amrud*
15. Mango	*Aam*
16. Plum	*Alubukhara*
17. Strawberry	*Strawberry*
18. Cherry	*Cherry*
19. Raspberry	*Rasbhari*
20. Black berry	*Black berry*
21. Litchi	*Litchi*
22. Papaya	*Papita*
23. Grape fruit	*Chakotra*
25. Jambu fruit	*Jamun*
26. Sweet lime	*Mausambi*
27. Lauqat	*Lauqat*
28. Musk melon	*Kharbooja*
29. Mulberry	*Shahtoot*
30. Custard apple	*Sharifa*